ACCESS AUSTRALIAN POETS: 1

SONGS OF A GOLIARD

This first edition is published in a limited run
of 750 casebound copies of which this is number

...........78............

Songs of a Goliard

Guy Weller

Illustrations & design by Melody Hampton

Acknowledgements

My thanks to Messrs. Routledge, 11 New Fetter Lane, London EC4, for permission to include Sidney Keyes' poem *Remember Your Lovers* in the Appendix to this volume.

Some of these poems first appeared in various publications, including *Westerly*, *Artlook*, *Pelican*, *The Australian Magazine* & *The Tippler*. Others were read at readings at The Stables (*Lip Service*) and The Maltings in Perth, La Paloma in Barcelona, and The Blue Monkey in San Francisco. Still others were sent as (unsolicited) epistles.

Ever grateful to Rod & Lyn Moran, John Harper-Nelson, Helen Weller, Carl Vine, Veronica Brady, Kim Rooney, Hal Colebatch, Martin & Meredith Bennett, Margaret Merrilees, Pete Lake, Angela Seward, Fran Balfour, Les Murray, Tim (TJ) Jones, my brother Archie and my grandfather A.N.G. Irving, all of whom have, at one time or another, encouraged my work, and assisted me signally thereat. And to Frank Devine, for his worship of words.

Published in 1997 by Access Press
PO Box 132, Northbridge, Western Australia 6865

National Library of Australia, Cataloguing-in-publication Data
WELLER, Guy: *SONGS OF A GOLIARD*
ISBN 0 86445 063 X

Dedication

to Melody Hampton

As ever you fetch me promise, my dove,
by the leaf in your beak's deft thrust,
you'll be mine 'til the seas run dry, my love,
and the mountains crumble to dust.

And I shall be thine, in this double exchange
of pleasure, and sickness, and health.
Your portion to waste, yours to arrange,
for you are my fortune, and wealth.

There's fault in our deed, I'll warrant you that,
but we've neither foreclosed on our Bill.
We've forgiven the tallies scrawled on the slat
when the debts grew too large to fulfil.

And these cancelled scores now litter our life
like old games we have won, and lost.
You have filled up my files, my darling wife,
with these scribblings of profit and cost.

But whatever in Heaven rules crossly above
will record this deed of our Trust,
which expires when the seas run dry, my love,
and the mountains crumble to dust.

"Marney"   *Melody Hampton*

Portrait of Marney

What would you, girl? On what do you softly dream
as you gaze so hopefully on life's rich feast?
For one so young, you seem so wise, so serene,
though sadness threads its solemn way through your eyes, at least.

You sweet and fragrant creature, fragile thing.
How you shame up all our action, all our strife.
What man alive would stagger on with his blustering
and swagger, if he could fold you in as his wife?

Should he but dare to tangle in such tensile silk,
and wrap him in such beauty, which might choke his air.
He'd be mad but to meet those eyes of floating milk
with aught but tenderness, and caress those wisps of hair.

I see you in the Alhambra, wrapped in brocade
of crimson and silver cunningly wrought, in slippers of gold;
wandering through bathhouse and fountain and sweetening glade
in the languid way of the spirit which grows not old

in joy's oasis, nay, nor partakes of decay.
Minstrels hover about you, and their songs murmurous run.
Petals float on the water, and on the soft banks of clay
you recline and bask at leisure, absorbing the sun,

as your soft, white body opens up like a flower
stretching its tendrils to the blazing presence above;
the water plashing about you, in this crystal bower,
a deliquescent symphony, a cascade of love.

Ah, girl. Thou art most beautiful, thou art dark
and shrinking lovely, and a soft assault to the eyes.
Thou art a garden, truly, a tree of delicate bark,
full fruitful in thy very glance of quiet surmise.

Foreword

These are occasional verses in both senses of the word. A number of them have been specifically written for occasions of greater or lesser dignity, whilst the balance have been put together occasionally over the years in a most goliardic fashion.

All of my poems were written to be recited aloud, since I am something of an addict to incantation. A number of them are songs written for plays, which may well lose something by being taken out of their context here.

Poetry is, or should be, the liqueur of language — wine distilled down and down to a sixth or a tenth of its original volume, with exotic additives and spices blended in. The sheer banality of much of the verse one encounters these days reflects, I think, a general weakness of stomach rather than of mind.

Discovering myself in the ridiculous position of being forty, I find it amusing to read over some of the frantic verse-prayers of my twenties — I have included one or two here as a small and highly personal historical record.

Did one really feel as strongly as all that, or was it all made up?

Can one take such raw intensity without a mitigating grain of salt, and a fleck or two of pepper?

And what about those who carry all this bombastic nonsense grimly on into their thirties, then their forties and fifties — is this some hectic exercise to remain forever young, forever passionate, forever irresponsible?

The really good poets study their somewhat ill-documented craft with passion, leaving the dissection of emotion to the night-club singers.

They do not rhyme parts, they clip their consonants and carefully separate their vowels or, when it is appropriate to group them, let them rumble with mimesis. They create hard little physical structures, not thoughts, or drifting mind-bubbles.

I am not a really good poet and, luckily, have no over-riding ambition to become so. I am a spare-time carver, whose scrapings and scratchings have, on occasions, brought happiness to a number of people, generally when such things are mixed up with generous servings of roast lamb, and a few bottles of fine old tawny port, or some such lubricant.

In any such process, one tends to borrow a mug of sugar, and a glass or two, from the guys next door. Where I have used the work of others for specific effect, I have tried to provide suitable reference, although invariably there will be some which have been overlooked. Others, perhaps, are unconscious.

I should hope that any such will be put down to oversight, or even ignorance, rather than subterfuge. References to, or echoes of, other poems, such as that in my *Carmen Melody* to the well-known image of Yeats (his "gong-tormented sea"), are designed to amuse, not to appal.

I have gathered here all those poems and tit-bits which seem to me to work on and off the page, and a few others which seem to me perfect rubbish, but which various friends have urged me to include, for differing reasons.

For this little publication is produced for those self-same friends, and for no others, unless they care to join that small band.

To the latter category, incidentally, all who are relaxed, sane and self-sufficient are welcome, whether I know them or not, and whether or not they have ever joined my less-than-luxurious table.

Poems written as mine have been (i.e. without purpose or design) are a form of table-talk, and it is usually late at night, half-drunk, and cheerily that they are read, or babbled.

If you prefer to read them silently, at least do so with a beaker of wine near to hand, a laugh somewhere about your lips, and a good joke lurking at the back of your mind.

That way, you will catch some of the bubbles in this muddled brew. But remember — do not try and drink too deep of such mixture, or you'll end with the dregs on your lips, since the pot is a crude one, and the wine not always of the finest.

If these little songs bring pleasure, they have done their merry job, and discharged their burden. If not, they can do no harm to a world already quite mad, and impervious to depredation from the likes of me.

Guy Weller, Sydney, 1997.

Contents

Songs from the Plays

Appendix

In Praise of Beauty

Assuredly, although beauty is momentary and fickle with the restlessness of the blood, as is the way of imaginary good, nevertheless it cannot be denied that it is good. For if whatever God has willed from all eternity is fair, then all that which hath a temporal fairness is, as it were, a mirror of the eternal beauty.

Guibert de Nogent, *De Vita Sua* (c. 1100 AD)

And In Memory of the Goliards

But these others, who served a ruinous altar and got a scanty living by it: the grammarians of Toulouse sitting up at nights to argue the frequentative of the verb to be: Rahingus of Flavigny filling his scanty leisure with copying Virgil: Froumund of Tegernsee collating manuscripts of Persius with chilblained hands: Primas shivering and mocking in his shabby cloak, writing a lament for Troy with Bacchanalian tears: the Archpoet coughing his heart out on the Lombard roads; a century of nameless vagabonds: on these the iniquity of oblivion hath blindly scattered her poppy.

They kept the imagination of Europe alive: held untouched by their rags and poverty and squalor the Beauty that had made beautiful old rhyme.

And for those of us who are the conservatives of letters, for whom literature obeys the eternal movement of the tides, for whom the heavens themselves are old, there remains the stark simplicity of Terence — "In truth they have deserved to be remembered of us."

> O no man knows
> Through what wild centuries
> Roves back the rose.

Helen Waddell, *The Wandering Scholars* (1927)

I Pagliacci

for John Bell

Put on the motley, the paint and the powder;
what does it matter now, this brief distress?
This halfwit fear, short flush of hope: one last caress
from you, my faithless, witless girl will devour
all my garish grief, all my anxious age
in one quick thrust of tilting, liquid song.
Why, o why did you leave me, in a crash of rage
like cymbals struck, or an old weird gong
rung into misery, a tired and stumbling chord
rumbling from instrument to instrument?
I am still a man, still heft my sword
however blunt or worn to fierce intent,
my painted lady, clown's sad joke, and life's bright toy.
Whom the gods laugh to embroider, they love to destroy.

Me pican los ojos de tanto mirarte

Miravet de Ebro, Spain, 1978

You trick my eyes when sting you lovely,
lady mine, you snip me smart.
I had pillaged all your feeling
and nibbling it, consumed it wholly:
now from hives of lonely dreaming
eyes like bees bewildered dart.

And like a bear with paws in honey,
with muddled greed, I slurping start,
as swarms of bitter words come winging,
prick my lips with wicked stinging,
love secreted plucks its levy
from the iris: o what bevy
beggars this, my rummaged art.

The Coat of Many Colours

The tale of Joseph and the coat of many colours as contained in Genesis is too well-known to need comment here. In this piece, however Jacob, or Israel, old and senile, imagines Joseph as the cause of death in childbirth of his beloved Rachel, making the gift of the coat a sort of blood-offering. In fact, of course, it was the youngest and fairest of Jacob's children, Benjamin, who was the culprit in this regard.

There, my son, I have had it woven, here is displayed
the cloak of all my love from the loom of my desire.
Your mother, God rest the soul of that gentle maid,
lives within this garment. Hers is the sparkle and the fire

rimmed in its glimmering hems. The women have laboured long
on this masterpiece, as they have never worked before.
It has trickled through God's fingers; it is itself a song
of thread and spindle, a hymn to her who lives no more,

no more, no more, Rachel mine, my darling bride,
my lasting peace, my fig-filled heaven, my fruitful girl,
o my garden! Let me huddle, let me hide
in the folds of this rich coat, let it billow, let it furl

its gold and silver threads about this wintry frame.
I am old and sick and foolish. I had hoped to love your son
with this mad gift, to cauterize the crazy pain
of your murder at our hands, we to become but one,

but one, but one. Your laughing lips lie in his face
like razors wedged, your eyes are sunken deep in his,
those cheeks are yours, roses sprung in a barren place,
your voice still lives, in him, in him! What you were, still is,

and what you were becoming now has been and lives
on and on in him, and now in this poor gift
of mine to you and him, my darling. He who gives
this fragile cloth drenched with gold from his wealth of thrift

2

says peace to the youth who killed the flower of his joy
as its bud burst, and blesses him who should be cursed.
Forgive me, frail ghost, I am entranced of the boy
who bears your soul within him. At the very worst

I can love him just as much as you, and that would mean
the vows I made upon your death have been fulfilled.
I spread the coat before me, the dazzle of its sheen
is endless, picking out this pattern which God has willed

in his wisdom: you, he, this silver thread, this gold.
I trick you into living for a moment, but my senses
ache with loneliness. You are gone, and I am old,
and all my artifice, all my cunning defences

against pain are dashed to pieces in a surge of grief.
Let this coat be daubed with blood, let the boy who wears it rue
the red day of his birth, may every snivelling thief
of love and honour, may your very brother turn upon you

and hurl you weeping to a shallow desert grave!
Let your murderous joy undo you, so that you understand
your birthright and its burden. Your bright wit will not save
you from your brethren, nor from God's remorseless hand,

or from Israel's, God-forsaken, God-forgotten.
O my sparkling boy, spawn of my desire,
my love's last roost! All that is withered, spent and rotten
sneers and spits at the memory of the faded fire

which begat thee, child of my love, mirror of my dreams.
This glory is yours, and hers. Do not soil its splendour.
Wrap it about your shoulders. Look how it shimmers and gleams!
Do not question its purpose, nor the joyful pain of its sender.

Pirate Lovesong

for Kim Rooney

Oír la noche inmensa, más inmensa sin ella
Pablo Neruda, Poema 20

The night remembers. Windlasses of stars
in thunderclaps of cloud are frothy turning,

tug me drenched in drink through Barcelona's
gleam of derrick, seething rigs of tapestry.

Sadness threading bluster with its tremor
flutes her thin from harboured churn of lee.

How I loved her: how she fathomed me
when half the winter wild pitched us burning;

how we sounded love, to raft us hungrily
in eyes of satin seas alive with yearning.

Listen to the night: how huge it is without her!
Kisses cling like dew of early morning

barely melted. Savage waters hiss and sing
as blue festoons of frost come pearly dawning.

Listen to the night. Distant chords are flung about
by some *borracho*, slopped to bed, still rollicking

his gusty song. Harmony is strung apart
with every shivered fleck come flickering

down wind's black spout. I know I love her not
though knowledge riddle all my reckoning:

love her, loved her not. A smile wrecked my heart
and littered deep that shallow lust of living

whilst I loitered, half with, half without her,
perplexed the half with love and half with bickering,

marooned us both, drifting through embraces
rough with squall in bodies' wanton giving;

set this craft such other cunning lovers
swart her seams, to quench that siren singing.

Done is done. Such treasure falls too easily
to ragged men who set the ports a-ringing:

should have hoarded, settled to the past,
left her early, let that grief go skimming

cross its current, green, green to the last
with weed swollen, lunge of power brimming;

but night could never blacken, sea excite
her sudden toss, nor wind dent its dinning

if ever memory stiffen, spend her tight,
or she be free, and not be worth the winning.

Hippie Girl Hitch-hiking

Why does she stare, swollen-bellied,
with eyes so sorrowing?

What seeds has she scattered,
What harvests yet to bring?

Lazarus Handled

Who, black and unhappy,
shriven of power
and weak as straw;
who scrabbles thus
in passion's greed
at my death's door?

Peace had I baffled witless
all this buffetsome life;
friends and hectic relations,
my fat, despairing wife;

and sank at last to my thin bed
determined never to rise;
curdled blood in an aching head,
snuffed my flickering eyes.

But no desire is single
nor ever pure.
I hear the sorcerer whisper
that dreaded cure

and heave, shrink as I will
am unravelled and unstrung;
life gripping at horror,
the well of fear sprung

dark, dark into screams of day
and the fickle, dubious mob,
wrung to a wild hosannah,
tricked to his eager love,

whose hunger for my carcase
I cannot kill.
The agate eyes of a miser God
kindle, wink me still.

Spider Night

I stayed for a while with friends in Bridgetown, in a little beaten-up caravan on their back block. During the night a large spider used to creep out and spin its webs around my few possessions. Some ghastly children came visiting, eventually, and crushed him with a shoe.

Soft struggle, spider, by my head tonight,
crept from all this tousled bed
and agog at the light,
with splintered eye unbuttoned,
silken soft, tincture of ash white,

knots and wriggles
eight bristling hairdoms
in little tugs of fright;
and o what pickle of a fang
pumps yellow driblets
blackwards into night!

Gone in a quick flick to his crevice there.
Harmless, soothes the book,
will be found everywhere
these Garden Wolves.

Nevertheless,
I'll carefully bed, Daniel,
and skirt your webs.
I have known you twist me in your spell
out of sight, when half dead,

and deck the silver shimmered air
with dark festoons of spite;
cloak the thrust of fantasy
at the queer pitch of delight.

Soft struggle, spider,
in the spindle of his dreams.
Warp the crackle of his body.
Spin him tiny screams.

The Death of Daniel

The children have crushed Daniel,
just like that.
Pashed him to a pulp
with one twig of a leg
left sadly poking.
Wham, splat!

You can't write elegies
for spiders,
and the children's fear
is not devoid of sense.

But what cherry of a fist
wrought this grisly spell?
Clutched that thick shoe
and, creeping upon innocence,
unleashed a bolt from hell:
thrashed poor Daniel
stickier'n goo?

Sonnet

The sun hangs over Crawley like a cauldron tipped,
the University simpers, smug and pure.
The river loiters along it. Nothing else moves
or has any destination. The trees stripped
of defences sulk in the sun, melting in yellow,
hiding their leaves. The peacocks in the garden
jerk their heads and listen to the silence.

They are reading Blake. Their little caves grow dim
and faces peer. A girl carefully farts.
The pages turn to the steady march of silence.
The sun tears at the foliage. Great ferns grip and cling.
Teeth chatter in a room. There is a smell of fear,
of flesh turning to stone. Hidden, high and clear,
heedless and barely heard, the giant cicadas sing.

Plantagenet Spring

*Henry II of England (and half of France by Duchy) was married to
Eleanor of Aquitaine, a most remarkable women, and a great patroness
of the arts. She deserved better than Henry, who eventually locked her up
for keeps. She mothered, amongst others, Richard Lionheart and John,
and her children made incessant war upon their father.*

For thirty years he wintered out his season,
freshly grizzled, and his walls dug in
against drifting unconcern. The fierce cold of his reason
belittled lust and sheathed what skittish passion
he could muster from his courtiers. Lord of the pain
he imposed on his gloomy fiefdom, he abhorred the sun
which far from his grip gleamed weak on his white demesne.

In a green rush she all but smothered him
and her lips jagged and snagged him back into living.
The flush of tears in the ice pearl of his eyes
was his life brimming, a frosted soul in an uproar of singing,
like a silly madcap strung and flung in the thing
within him, unaware that on all sides and about him
this earth that he thought was his heaved with her kin.

The Accountant

Scratching at these figures on the page,
my mind clicking where the ink would clot.
Lives hang on this guesswork. My own does not,
but I am unimportant. Like frightened armies
column falls upon column in a helpless rage.
Nothing really balances: each sweet series
of nonchalant poise is soon plucked undone.

I portion out their livings, every one,
he who is cost-efficient, he who is not.
Vizier of these kingdoms, hung in a royal cage
and set to toil for the hard-eyed men whose theories
I must suffer, rectify and still assuage.
I am the abacus, which never wearies
of futility as beads hum to their slot.

In Flanders Fields

For A.N.G. Irving, my grandfather, who served with the AIF in France in 1915-1917, was wounded there, and to that madness lost his brother Herbert, to whom he wrote a moving poem: "For we're leaving France behind us, and half my heart is there." He was a fine poet, and a greatly civilized man. His poem "Poppy Day", which inspired this piece, is attached at the end of this collection, as is his elegy "The Dead".

Their revels now have ended: look, they are none
who stormed and battered, shrieking.
In such conquest all reason is undone
and either party now lies reeking.

Strange how pomp drew them here
in their millions, smartly buckled,
all tricked with the odds. Chuckled
into tinny anger, though, they hid their fear

in mighty shouts of almost genuine rage
and rushed like silly roosters to their doom.
Most of them were drowned. From another age,
bogged cannon, unattended, simply loom.

In London, too, the festive season over,
French is felt to have blundered, and is removed.
Art potters under Bloomsbury cover
and economic theories are improved.

Somewhere in Flanders the last shudder
of the last soldier shivers, and is gone.
The great armies, shorn of their human rudder
are headlines merely, screaming *We Have Won*!

But the victor's littered skull is bent awry,
and grins as it sips at the gently sucking mud.
Such a queer, feeble peace. Not a single cry
along ruined rivers, gangrenous with blood.

He puts his heart (and his soul) into business

I set my soul an evil task,
and asked him follow after me,
I forced him take my leering mask
and sup with me, and dine with me.

To commerce bleak I cozened him,
and the icy wind of business drear.
With pimps and cheats I peopled him,
and with croaks of greed I bent his ear.

And he was appalled at what he saw,
and whispered quick in my thick red ear:
"Let us begone from this field of war
where none is the victor, and naught doth cheer!"

But, fool that I was, I sneered at him,
and upbraided him, and his formless fears.
I asked what he thought had supported him,
and filled up his belly, and lent him his years.

I reminded him how we had struggled together
through deserts of want, and yearned for the feast;
How gnarled we had come, and bitter with weather
vowed out our revenge — or survival, at least.

How we'd struck up our pact, that we'd never again
be the flotsam that floats on the river's soft mud.
Sell our brains up for coin from unspeakable men
who would chew on our learning, but to spit out its cud.

But he gazed at me long, and the tears on his cheek
glistened like pearls in the tides of the sun.
And his fingers stretched out, so to stop me speak
as he brushed my lips with his golden glove.

> *And he whispered me soft: "You have deeded and done*
> *what was ruin to us both. You have mortgaged love."*

The Drovers' Cook

for the 'Two Bloody Poets', Roger Montgomery and Peter Capp

O the drovers' cook is a dreary cove,
and the thick, black, merciless stew
which he ladles with glee from his bushman's stove
can sure make a mess of you.

The one I mean is old Charlie Sheen,
who roams the Condamine.
Takes squatters' pay for his filthy day
at his pots of dogshit and slime.

His pig-eyed look has the divil's squint,
and his nose is all blistered and mean.
His chin wrinkled up like arse-cloth lint.
Yes, that's our Mister Sheen.

There's a tale we used to tell of him,
us bludgers of the line.
He was rumoured to have had a fling
up round the Condamine.

'Course, that were forty year off,
before we cut our horse.
They say he used to be a toff
from Engel-and, or worse.

They say he came here arter gold,
and struck it too, what's more.
Had a mansion full of servants bold
up Sydneyside North Shore.

And a monster spread, on these here plains,
where the prickly poisons grow;
getting cattle-thick after every rains,
building his fortune slow.

You wouldn'ta thort that our old cook
could've lived the life of a swell!
The bloody old snivelling bad-tempered crook
with his pottage broiled up in hell.

But they say that he did, and no wealthier prick
Resode on the Condamine.
Canapes before dinner, and the bleeding pick
of the world's most delicious wine.

And it's said that a flighty country lass
turned his head in a horrible way.
He could buy all he craved, but this one, alas,
bore a perilous price, they say.

She was hot in the way that Australian girls are,
but could dimple and coo with the best.
She sneered at his money, but I'll bet you a jar
she'd totted it up to the test.

She married him, sure, after stringing it out
as long as she decently could.
And he opened his purse as he'd opened his heart
and she struck as a woman would.

In Sydney she preened like an Indian Queen,
not a lass from the Condamine.
And the Honourable Charles Bousanquet Sheen
was her bottomless Aztec mine.

And because he was careless in this, she supposed
he was blind in everything.
A dashing young captain from Home arose
to her delicate simpering.

And they say that old Charlie — yes, him over there,
a-spitting into our pot.
Came upon them one night, all sweaty and bare
and killed the affair with a shot.

There's a law amongst men who are decently wed,
which the judge would have honoured, in part.
But Charlie's mad shot at the skunk in his bed
took his girl in the heave of her heart.

Away he was took, to the dungeon and hook,
and he served out his time without fuss.
But the bastards in there taught the cunt how to *cook*,
and he takes his revenge on us.

I've a soft spot for Charlie, despite of the spew
which he serves up with hard, chunky bread.
I can nibble his damper, and pick at his stew
and pretend I've been solidly fed.

All day in the saddle, rounding up cows,
you develop a taste for beef.
So there's something inspired in a cook who vows
that it's mutton or nothing, you thief!

I could cut one out of the bellowing pack
and slither its throat in a trice!
The boss is in Sydney, and ain't coming back
to this bogwash of maggots and lice.

But I s'pose the old bastard he pays as his cook
has a mission from out of his past.
I doubt if he's paid to ensure nothing's took
but just does it, and will to the last.

It must have been tough, in Van Diemans Land,
and I've seen the thick scars on his back.
As hard as it hurts, I'll give him my hand
and a share in our babble and yack.

Bloody old turd! Poor old bastard. Look:
he's hell's own chef, I'm agree'n.
Be-elzebub couldn't *shit* a worser cook!
But *I'll* chew yer munga, Mr Sheen.

Claddagh

for the band Claddagh, Sydney, 1995

In the Cricketers' Arms, down the strip of Balmain
there's a band with a fiddler, an Irish crew,
There's a hot little tap-room, where on Thursdays they play
for the lost and the lonely, and the passers-through,

and a handful of locals, who haunt this place
with a grim dedication, half desperate, half cheer;
as if music might magically turn their face
from this orgy of chance, and its watery beer,

     As she plucks at her fiddle, and plays.

There's an Irishman fresh out of Dublin, it seems,
with the sweet, canting lyric so kin to his race,
On the keyboard a tall, sallow girl wearing jeans
with shimmering hands, and a soft, listless face;

There's a pudgy old songster, with cavernous belly,
a voice sweet as honey, rich to the tongue,
and the fiddler, her face from a lost Botticelli
fretting and bouncing their music along

     As she slices her fiddle, and plays.

There's a magic come over the Cricketers' Arms
on a Thursday night, in its hot little hall.
There's a music which quickens, as swift as it charms,
the blood of the mob which it holds in its thrall:

The insect-thin lass who has downed too much Guinness
propelled by the music to fidget and jerk
to the laughter of all, applause at the finish
for the skimbleshanks dance she contrives to work;

and the drunk from the outback, pushed by the song
to windmill his limbs in a dustcloud of dance;
The fiddler smiles as she winds him along
the tunnelling tunes of her Celtic trance

As she rollicks her fiddle, and plays.

And I think of the fiddler of Dooney, and others,
who have harped on the strings of their harmony's toy,
brought tears to the eye of old fathers and mothers
adrift in this ocean of tears and joy,

Who have nurtured the songs and laments of their forebears
through centuries of struggle, and shuddering strife
as a man from the mines, enslaved to his labours
shepherds his pittance home to his wife.

The band is electric with well-rehearsed numbers
from Dublin, and Manchester, London and Cork;
The Cricketers' Arms comes an Atlas of wonders
and shoulders the world on its yielding stalk

As she stretches her fiddle, and plays.

There's a music which flutters direct from the heavens
as if God wanted laughter, God wanted song,
'Tis found in the world's little hothouse taverns
where the losers accrete in their slobbering throng.

There's a lilt to that aria no opera can capture
nor concert hall pin to its rich, velvet walls,
it's a violin string just teased into rapture
it's a song full of bathos, a song which appals,

a song full of anger, and history's complaint,
a working man's cry to be freed from his yoke,
from hands chapped and weary, from a heart grown faint
from a lifetime of toil, and from life's mirthless joke,

yet a song which is ever a shudder of beauty
and a thing which despite its own misery, sings.
Along with our rage sits a strange sense of duty
to liven our lives with these sonorous hymns

As she cradles her fiddle, and plays.

In the Cricketers' Arms, down the strip of Balmain
there's a band with a fiddler, an Irish crew,
There's a hot little tap-room, where on Thursdays they play
for the lost and the lonely, and for passers-through,

There's an Irishman fresh from old Eire, it would seem,
with the sweet, canting lyric so kin to his race,
On the keyboard a girl from some willowy dream
with shimmering hands, and a soft, wistful face

and a Melchior fat, with tavern-rich belly,
his voice thick as honey, sweet to the tongue,
and the fiddler, her face from some lost Botticelli
laughing and teasing their music along

      As she plucks up her fiddle, and plays.

His Elderly Wife

for John Harper-Nelson, whose home was invaded, whilst he sat at hearty lunch in nearby Northbridge, by Brownshirts from the Main Roads Department who came to dig tunnels beneath his house and home.

He was a bubble of energy — burst him, and you'd see
there was but air and froth about, or that's what they said.
His chest was round, like a barrel. He thrust it out, at strife
when it happened, like when drillers came to his house
to muckle his garden, and push him out. The Main Roads people.
He was alone in this bureaucrats' Battle o' Bulge
apart from his loping grandsons, and elderly wife.

God, he got angry! They had come during lunch
in a wine-sloshed Northbridge tavern, where he had fed.
He returned to a nightmare of drilling through his privacy
of garden-mulch, and cunning path. An uprush of mud
sploshed over all his fiddlings with his shrubs and trees.
That they should dare! That they should turn the knife
in the muscle of his pleasure, and that of his elderly wife!

He rang the Press. He'd friends there, of course,
having newsed the ABC for twenty years.
He was so bloody cross! In all his upright life
he'd fairly dealt, assuming that was best.
The ghosts of Trinity College swarmed to him here
and urged him on to decency. But this chaotic mess
in the garden uncivilised him, and his elderly wife.

An Englishman flees to his castle, a Scot to his crags,
and the lumpy army opposite is obliged to tunnel.
It hopes that the walls will cave in, that its dumb advance
will be quickened by this burrowing. It is nuisance
that inhabitants cling hard to their huts, that drum and fife
will not clear them on sounding, to shoot out the funnel
of convenience. Certainly not him, nor his elderly wife.

He has seen it all, old warrior, and now must dress anew
in the motley armour left him, drag his sword from the wall.
When he'd set it all behind him, this war of the world
and sunk into retirement, for to publish books.
They have crept up from behind him, angry at a life
slipped past their planning structures, and their petty hooks.
They will out-tunnel him, and his elderly wife.

Spring Morning

Green moss clings with strawberry smells.
The sheer delight of things in things!

He hopes for life in the far reaches of the night

Do not die
little mothinsect thing
seemingly stuck
in this white waste
of paper;
you have just lost years
of your tiny life
wiping your legs
bobbing your head
untucking your wing
and fluttering,
heaving to
and teetering
in absurd haste.

If you die
I shall have to go to bed
huge and yawning.
The morning creeps with her hot, red eye
and will pick you in fingers
of chiselled light
into feathery bits,
small many-leg,
spawn of the night,
malingering.

Never Happy

Pompilius sighs, for life is short,
and all he attempts is crabbed and wrong;
Yet time hangs heavy. He is out of sorts
and frets and cries, for the day is long.

Burswood Casino

for W.H. Auden

More than their hands are living, their eyes are attracted
to this riot of chance in a world without dance or song.
Ashamed even of daring, even guile is distracted
by a fell doom, rung like a mournful gong.

They know they will lose their pittance — nay, have lost it all
a thousand times, and will lose it all again.
They curse and mutter softly, but the talk is pinched and small
like the cries of wandering cripples. They seem shrivelled men

who gather to this feast of velveteen despair.
Luck is their single condiment, that too is thin;
and even hope is stunted, for this poor life can spare
only tangled blackjacks — always the two on the ten,

aces falling together to mock success.
They bob on a sunless ocean in their small and fragile ships.
The wizened dealer, his hands in a flickering caress
feeds like a fiend on their small hoard of chips.

In a stable, ordered world it seems they are mad
to gamble so, such playthings for the gods.
A preposterous courage steers them on, however sad,
able yet to threaten fate, and defy the odds.

Perhaps it is true that they really have no fear,
setting sail for freedom, not all forlorn;
perhaps some spark of booty-dream is buried here,
some savage sea-wolf struggling to be born

from the bloodied womb of hope, and youth and joy.
They grin at their tiny plunder, when it is won,
and laugh at their glistening luck, like the fisherman's boy
who shouts as he hauls at his nets, and scoops up the sun.

The Good Ship Maltings

Written upon the occasion of the launch of The Perth Artists Club at The Maltings in Perth, November, 1992, and recited to a motley crew of poets, artists, drunkards and fools gathered at that establishment.

Welcome all, to this poor ship,
welcome sailor, henchman, foe,
welcome all yon fellowship,
well-to-come, and well-to-go;

Do not fear the wind in the sails
nor the furious winter rages,
Here are folk to tell you tales,
artists, poets, tumblers, sages,

Here are drunkards, vagabonds, thieves,
Here are blacktoothed gypsy ghouls,
Here no pardons, by-your-leaves,
Here are freaks, and here are fools.

Should this lot inspire alarm
in gentle breast and ordered mind,
remember dreams ne'er did no harm
to angel, god nor humankind.

For all is dream, in this poor ship,
no business grim can enter here,
nor commerce thin, nor theory grip
at pleasure's throat, to throttle cheer.

Here let wit and laughter wed,
let games and nonsense rule the roost,
let little weight be on what's said,
let Edward Lear displace old Proust;

And Rabelais teach Eliot
where to stuff his Margate woe;
we'll talk of footy if we wot
or bloody Michelangelo!

In short, let joy awaken gloom
to join the dance of simple folk,
let mind's sharp pain bring forth its bloom,
and fancy free, unlace the yoke

of moral virtue, all that's right:
good jobs, good deeds, good laundered thoughts,
good politics, good deals, good sorts,
good wives, good blokes, good God, goodnight.

Come slip the knot, you stevedores,
we've been ashore too long, God's oath!
we'll fetch such jewels from magic shores
to dazzle maid and matron both

and set our craft athwart the tide
of sour spite, thick stream of fear;
let humour swell, let wit abide
to warm the spars and rafters here.

So button up, you pirate dudes,
in this poor ship we'll live with swank;
we'll shock the godly, keelhaul prudes,
and puritans can walk the plank!

Loll in comfort round the wardroom,
puff your baccy, down your rum,
forget you've ever seen a boardroom,
tell dirty jokes, admire a bum;

and sail with us to milky seas
alive with light from the glancing sun,
lets make a cure of life's disease
and fill our holds with sparkling fun.

So welcome all, to this poor ship,
welcome sailor, henchman, foe,
welcome all yon fellowship,
well to come, and well to go.

Morning After

Observed Myrtle in an early light
that his breath seemed thin;
his nose more splayed than it seemed last night,
less grip to his chin,

and more or less disliked him
now, though much too late.
A walloping spell of riot
had quite settled fate,

and her bare chill had melted
in one great stew of a kiss;
friends, and her clutch of relations,
were idle sport to this:

this rank howl of together
wrung from mortgaged lips,
wharving a palpable future
tightly amid their ships.

She knew a house they could live in,
would demonstrate, later today.
Plans whizzed in from the kitchen
and scrambled eggs on a tray;

and though they were infants in passion,
she felt even *Pix* would say
that Love had fostered a lesson
no nuptial truth could repay

and what about *him*, eh?

He, with all the charm he could exert
certainly didn't doubt her,
but washed him spotless, smiled himself to work
and forgot all about her.

Hunting Accident, 1828

Her mind is decked with cobwebs
where the spider is the fly;
the hunter is the hunted,
her shrivelled lips, an eye;

his spick red suit a smear of blood,
his foaming words a lie;
the gleaming spurs she hoards with love
that he may not die.

Gold sank in his ruined face
like a vicious king.
But braided dreams can not erase
her rank misgiving,

living, thus, with him;
felt sharp hairs tickle her,
and tiny fang which rammed in
made merry with her

delicate emotions.
Faun he felt her. This was gentle
of him. When he rode, though,
she was furiously alone

in love's tumble, self her horses,
the steel ribs which streaked her,
and o what whips of hatred beat her
then, what mind's bridle

loosed her mad careering
and hot wealth of embraces,
sore of the saddle, stung in the thing:
kicked, tipped over the traces,

chasing *him*, stark, impotent prey.
He, gurgling the thorn
in his throat's thick horn
lay frothing away.

Which loss she treasured, mind having caught her:
the dolorous mouth which glazed upon
such struggle ended; her wasted portion
and gloomy widow's pleasure — all, all they had taught her

tamed her, arranged her very nicely
for the self-same endeavour
with her wry wiles. How to coax any other
comfort hither, how to be loved, precisely?

Wrapped in the fragile tissue
of the spider and the fly,
the hunter seeks its issue
with bulbous glaze of eye.

By Candlelight

The flame ambles on the candlewick
and sucks at the air
in quick gulps. With frantic wings
and the dark desire
of cradle night
the grey moth flutters
whisker feathers
on her soft rim of light.

He rears to attention
with a brief stutter of joy,
preens in this private breeze,
pleased and coy,

and swoops unseen from his height
with kindled fire;
carelessly wraps his proselyte
in her tiny pyre.

Let not those feet

Wm. Blake's great hymn popularly known as "Jerusalem" is to be outlawed from its hymnal by the Church of England. The reasons given, by the Rev. Rbt. Gray cover various crimes including City vs Country discrimination, and general inappropriateness to the modern age.

Let not those feet in modern time
Walk upon England's mountains green.
Lead hence the holy Lamb of God
Lest we fleece him naked, and pick him clean.

Did ever Countenance Divine
Shine forth upon these clouded hills?
Did they hazard their Jerusalem
Among these bleak Satanic Mills?

We must no longer sing of such,
Discriminate betwixt Country and Town.
Nor dream of Angels, nor anything much
Which might inadvertently bring us down.

Our God is now a paltry thing:
We have tugged off His tinsel crown.
He is a wisp like us — o, let us sing
The normalcy of Him, whom we've outgrown.

Let fall to rust my Bow of gold
And blunt my Arrows of desire,
And let the local Museum enfold
My useless Chariot of fire.

Let our hymns leave none in any doubt
That we have shrivelled Spirit up
And bottled him, and corked the spout
That all slop equal in the one plain Cup.

It is time to cease from Mental Fight
And soothe the sword to sleep in our hand.
We have no need of Jerusalem
In our grey and foggy, liberated land.

Back in the Saddle

for my brother Archie Weller

When yer down on the ground, to the terrible sound
of the rock smacking into yer head;
When yer body feels like it's been strung on a spike,
and yer wish ter Christ you was dead;

An' yer horse buggers off with a thundering hoof
and the ants come and nibble yer ear;
and you lie there and curse in yer rich stockie's verse
at yer luck in this prick of a year;

Then its back in the saddle again, old chook,
take the reins of the bridle once more.
Jiggle yer buttocks, and give 'em that look
yer supposed to be famous for,
        and stick it up 'em, Charlie.

When the women make mock of yer criss-crossed stock,
and suggest you are bruised, black fruit.
When they laugh at yer gait, and the squint of yer hate
as they sneer at yer primitive root.

And the one who yer've paid to be nobly laid
laughs as she fingers yer cock.
And washes it clean with her hands so keen
to finger yer wallet and sock;

Then its back in the saddle again, old chook,
take the reins of the bridle once more.
Jiggle yer buttocks, and give 'em that look
yer supposed to be famous for,
        and stick it up 'em, Charlie.

When the boss gives yer shit fer the hell of it,
and threatens to dock yer pay.
An' yer told the whole mob has gone loose on the job
while yer've dithered around in play;

And yer black, splotchy face is a sheer disgrace
and a dark confession of sin.
A man without place, or history or race,
the shit of a wandering gin;

Then its back in the saddle again, old chook,
take the reins of the bridle once more.
Jiggle yer buttocks, and give 'em that look
yer supposed to be famous for,
   and stick it up 'em, Charlie.

Portrait of Pompilius as a Young Man

A sound, if rowdy, mob. Idlers, philosophers, bums,
come rollicking round my fireside, and guzzling my wine.
They made me shake with merriment, rapscallion swine:
Ah, a fellow was rich in the ordurous pitch of such rascally chums.

Old Shovel there, and Choofer too, who painted his dick
with luminous paint, at a romp we had, and danced the throng
of my darkened guests lit up by the gleam of his luminous dong.
He's a Senator now, and keeps tight guard on his famous prick.

And Tubby, Diddlewit, Buddha, Lurch, and the boisterous crew
of hilarious youth, with wine stewed black in their belly's pot.
How we giggled at girls, between us, and their fertile rot!
When wit got drenched and soggy, then a pair of good tits would do.

Climbed, now, the whole pack of them, to careers and hopes,
and wives in the suburbs, children to feed, and mortgaged woe.
No laughter now, when we meet, just gloom spreading slow
round the distant sparkle of memory's fires, on the lower slopes.

"Would you care to have a lolly?" said the Captain of the Push,
"I wouldn't mind the black one," said the Person from the bush,
Then the Pushites all took counsel, saying, "Golly, but he's game.
"Let's make him our facilitator, he'll live up to his name."

So they took him down to Paddington, that Person from the bush,
And they granted him all privileges appertaining to the Push.
But soon they found his little ways more than they could stand,
And finally the captain thus addressed his little band.

"Now listen here, my brethren dear, for here's a jolly show,
"At every kind of house-disrupt this joker is a pro!
"He won't wash up nor sit the kids nor weed the vegie plot,
"He drinks our tea, steals our rice, and eyes our girls a lot."

So down in Jones' Fish-Cafe the members of the Push
Laid a dark and dirty ambush for the Person from the bush.
But against the wall of the Coffee Pot, the Person made a stand,
A drippy grin upon his lips, a *Herald* in each hand.

They sprang upon him in a bunch, but one by one they fell
As he whirled the furled-up newsprint with a liberated yell,
Till the sorely-battered Captain, with his leather shirt all torn,
Reared a head all smeared with gel in a manner most forlorn.

"You simply awful person," sobbed the Captain of the Push,
"Go back to Parramatta, or somewhere up the bush;
"And I hope that really shocking things soon occur to you,
"May you catch the you-know-what from a simpering you-know-who.

"May your stomach gas rise daily from the awful pooh you eat,
"May your underpants have skidmarks larger than your feet,
"May you drink a glass of Tooheys, mistaking it for beer,
"May the next push *you* impose on pierce your shitty ear.

"May mosquitoes bite your armpit, may pimples dot your face,
"May horrible little crawly things emasculate your race,
"Then when you're in a real tizz, a snivelling bitchy wreck,
"May you stuff the *Sydney Herald* down your slimy little neck."

Daily News: For the Record

Mrs Duckham, Mrs Joyce Duckham
of Geraldton, gathered a file
of neighbours' conversations,
mostly filthy, rattling decency
in its very lair
unwholesomely;
collected, too, photographs (huge)
depicting the squalor
of the urban aborigine
down Boulevard Duckham.
Convened the press, declared

(*Daily News, Perth, Australia, July 13, 1973, p.2*):

> "I'm not blaming the aborigines. They've been pushed into a
> community whose standards of behaviour and hygiene they are not
> ready for yet. It's not their fault."

And, directly overleaf:
Grandma Offers to Pay Thief
(for return of car stolen, pillar-box red,
immaculate condition, 1968 mod.,
Cortina, No. VZC 402).
Herein is featured Grandma
in slippers and gown, her hair all wisps,
year-laden, nipped with loss
yet wry with wreaths of smiles.
(It was not hers).
Dismay at Tax Bar on Charity.
Road Death Toll a Secret Thrill?
Train Jumps Rails — 25 dead.
Portuguese Napalm Atrocity (alleged).
Andy Capp, advertisements,
kaleidoscopic lead.

Pincushion head. Words intersect electrically,
slice and wedge. What profit aught
in a weird world, what can be taught
but reportage, when such crazy poetry
is daily laid to bed?

Spring Song

for Melody

When the rain comes sheening its magic over
our ramshackle home, with its snuggled fire;
and the flowers hang heads all laden with water
and clench up their beauty in hoarded desire;

When the sky is a canvas of shuddering oil,
when the frost is afoot, and wind's witches howl,
when the world splashes weary to wet winter's toil,
when there's mud in the hallway, and weather is foul;

It is then that a bud shows its brave shoot of leaf,
the sun struggles through, in its watery way
to dapple with gold the silver-black street,
and sizzle old beggars with shimmering ray.

And it's then that the birds begin fussing and plucking
their feathery breasts, and to hazard their song;
First a carol, alone in the water-logged air
then an answer, a chorus of gathering throng,

and Spring comes to life in everyone's heart
like a flower sprung up from its drooping despair,
like the circus has come, with its mad, cunning art
to out-riddle death, and enliven the air.

And it's then that my love is born once anew
like the godlings of old, which they buried in grief
to mourn them together, a whole season through,
that the cycle might turn to its blessed relief.

Through my long winter's night you have lain like the seed
buried within, with its green shoots outcrept,
and ever again, at the season decreed
you burst from the earth, where you have but slept.

I can picture the peasants, at each harvest's end,
clustered together, to schedule their woe;
that the world revolves thus, that pleasure should wend
so swiftly to anguish, and return so slow.

Now the sun is a-trickle across our small garden;
You are alive, and warm in my bed,
and I'll plant there a crop which will thicken and harden
to revive the embrace of the quick and the dead.

O my darling, my Springtime, my flowersome earth,
how you curl up my Winter, and shrug off its spite!
How my harvest is full: from that dreadful dearth
springs a riot of colour, and soft, swaying light;

and the small robin redbreasts puff as they skite
and the magpies soar high in the winnowing skies,
the sun like a blanket of thick, woollen white
lies draped over all in a sleepy surmise.

And I know that come Winter will come the lament,
and we'll slip from the light into cold, frozen dirt,
our sunlit liaison all scattered and spent,
and briefly apart, we will lie there inert.

But there isn't a power which can hold us forever
locked out of this living, out of this love,
our whiskery seeds will lock tendrils together
and in passion's short season, thrust sprouting above.

Pompilius in Parliament

Damn them for putting me here! I have no liking of,
nor desire to serve, my constituents. I was told it was fun
to sit in state, have secretaries, and muck about with words.
Now I'm caught in messy plots, and must affect to love
this faction leader or that, whilst the other I must shun.
A pox upon this hogs' latrine! They are all turds.

A Song for Mr Eliot

You grow old, Mr Eliot, in your grey lull,
and getting older, grow damned dull.
But there's an answer, even for you,
and here is what we shall do.
You will wear the bottom of your trousers rolled
and be made to walk all day upon the beach.
For sustenance, we shall supply a peach
and lemonade. You must endure, must be bold,
and if you hear what sounds like mermaids singing,
or scent their allure in the white foam springing
about your ankles, do not get too anxious:
just come and tell us all. Yes, tell us all
about it. And we shall listen to your ballyhoo,
despite the fact we know that they will never sing for you.

In Praise of Sheep

for the Merino

I.

In my opinion, Captain Bligh
was far too bad to write about.
But John McArthur and his rams
may justly move our ample hams
to rustic jigs of healthy joy,
for he bred sheep which thrive on drought!

Now *there's* a bloke to skite about.

II.

Ah, flint-eyed ram, hide inch-thick,
great pouch a-jiggle
with swarms of sheep!

And you, ewe. You too.

Carmen Melody

Away to our mountains, my threepenny sixpence lady,
come dance with me in my threadbare halls.
Let gypsies swarm, let all that is dark and shady
patch us a picture on our crumbling walls.

God knows I have loved you cheaply, o my little,
with spindthrift scarves and raggedy shawls;
How stingy seems your recompense, and how brittle
is the music which my spirit calls.

Would that I could fling a greasy hand
high in the air, and laugh with your song;
would that I could even half understand
the line of your life, the form that makes you strong,

gypsy mine, laughing and dancing, tricking me
and loving me, and twisting me, and trusting:
so much accepting, altogether shocking me
from the listless life which comes heaving and thrusting

out of the blackness, wish encrusted, fire in the ice
of splintered desire; yes, gypsy, mocking me
in my manhood, in my shrivelled hoard, and my slight vice;
the crazy loon within me, bursting free.

So off, off, to our crimson sparkling mountains
lush as velvet, trinketed with pearls;
lilies drooping in the cool splash of fountains,
yellow arching in rich, dark swirls,

as my love curls from the dark, o my darling,
to brush with limpid petals the thick skin of night.
Whirl for me, spin and weave in the gloaming
gypsy lover, remember me tight

in the history of your dance, let the glancing light
flame your crystal eyes to a ghastly red;
You are ablaze within me, you are mine tonight
in this rose-tormented, all-engorging bed.

Consuming Love

for Buenaventura Durruti, and for the old ones in Miravet de Ebro, who remember him, albeit dimly

Every child becomes old, at night,
when it dreams of the angels above;
and every man a soaring poet
when he whispers to whom he loves.

Let his voice be so sickly and weedy,
let the dream be of tinsel, or worse,
there's a hunger which renders us greedy
for heaven's insatiable verse.

A man without love is a danger
to all of the rest of his tribe.
To them, he's a castoff, a stranger,
'twere better by half that he died.

And knowing that he is but a bubble,
a skin casing nothing but air,
he fills up the void of his trouble
with the hatred of bitter despair.

His dreams are the screams of the tortured,
his delights are his shuddering lusts.
No one to share his misfortune,
no one alive whom he trusts.

And he clutches the tinpot insignia
of deathshead, *fascia*, and crown.
He is power's own paraphernalia.
He is awfully hard to bring down.

You will find him on every committee,
heading it up, if he might.
He will scoff at the cynically witty
for stepping aside from the fight.

And to art he'll turn, like a soldier,
He'll paint, spew out verses and songs,
he'll be critic, curator, crusader,
and righter of everyone's wrongs.

He will know that his songs are like croaking
of crows — cackling, and sad.
His music a throttled choking.
He will know that his poems are bad.

But this will not blunt his endeavour,
nor lighten the load of his lies;
loveless, forlorn, merely clever,
like a bell, he will toll 'til he dies.

He's a mind of his own, he's our Leader,
he's a tyrant, and scourger of sin.
Christ Jesus, omniverous saviour,
try sharpening your teeth upon him!

Sydney Harbour

for Tim (TJ) Jones, my drinkin' buddy

Silver streaks the aqua blue like steel ribbing
and the bridge floats above all, like half a frown.
Ferries bubble along, small splotches of green,
and yachts as white as swans go drifting down
this oil-drenched canvas.
The surreal beauty of the harbour
is washed with a pickling of light, through dappled clouds,
as if brush had been dabbed and jabbed in a frenzy
of ochreous yellow, hot to the touch,
a riot of colour-love, by a one-eyed man,
stocky before his easel,
with tilted head, squinting at the sun,
spreading a glorious skin of paint
with the thick slab of his thumb.

Moomintroll and Little My

for poor little Chay

*Tove Janson's delightful children's book series involving Moomintroll
and his family in Moominvalley (with the nasty Little My providing a
touch of acid) is, I think, amongst the finest work for children ever
written. I came across a child recently who had not been introduced to
this wonderland, which deprivation I consider a form of child abuse,
perhaps explained (but not excused) by the fact that her otherwise doting
parents are poets and artistes themselves. This minor calamity has
somewhat strengthened my view, which is a twist upon Plato's, that
poets (and philosophers for that matter) should not be encouraged to
breed, or not, at least, with one another.*

Said Moomintroll to Little My:
"The world is growing little."
And shook his head, and with a sigh
said: "Greatly so, and brittle."

"I am not happy just to stroll
and dither in my garden;
my tiny flock of fowl control
with unremitting feedin';

"In short, I'm full of discontent
as I grow crudely larger;
I wonder where my childhood went
and when I crossed the border."

But Little My just wagged her hips
(for boys did not impress her),
and tossed her locks, and pursed her lips
with supercilious pressure:

"The world is *vast*, you witless youth,
us being small just proves it;
Beyond these hills, the canyon Truth
just gapes at that which moves it,

"And all the earth is shuddered loose
by forces we but dream on;
your stupid flowers, hens and goose
but gags to what we scream on,

"and on, and on, through night's black noise
and frights we dare not utter;
You're growing up, you silly boy,
and now you'll *hugely* suffer!"

"No, no," said Moomintroll at last
when given turn of speaking;
"My mind ran not so slick or fast —
I was really only squeaking .....

"It's just that as I grow, it shrinks,
this oyster world of mine;
the pearl I cherished through its chinks
seems but a speck in brine,

"And I would love to *littler* grow,
not grumpier and bigger;
to laugh more softly, make *less* show,
not sit about and snigger

"with all you kids, as you forsake
our tiny pleasure fort,
where pain and age were beaten back
and liquid love was thought."

Found in the diary of Richard Potts, shearer

If ever I should lose this book,
and you, perchance, should find it,
remember, Richard is my name,
and *Potts* trots on behind it.

Mr Micawber takes his tea

for my old friend, and most delightful enemy, Avon Lovell

Ah, my dear, I see that we have guests.
Sssh! Down in the parlour. Men with papers.
I expect they have come with their lugubrious lists
of my various business debts. Let them sit awhile,
and enjoy short roost in the home of a gentleman.
We are not messy chandlers, nay, nor twopenny drapers
to usher 'em up in fear. Anyways, I hardly can
accommodate 'em. Thank'ee, m'dear: chamomile.

Eh, this rich, strong brew! How my nostrils ping
at the stench of it, and how it bunches my belly!
And what a brisk, clean morning it is. Makes a man sing
as he sets to his business a-twirling his stick at the birds.
I've a project afoot, m'dear, and expect a profit
of significant sort. There is something stale, and smelly
what floats up these stairs - I expect 'tis the distilled wit
of the bibulous bailiffs gathered below in their herds.

'Tis a goodly slurp, this beverage. Hast any more?
How sad that my ventures have so far come to naught.
Yet they should not hound me so! God's oath, I have swore
my very jacket away to these scallywags!
Would they strip me now like a strumpet scrag, and scrounge all
the tiny worth of my house, and my little fort?
A pox upon their mutterings! Let them bawl
their threats in the very street, like angry hags.

Yes, sugar, my love, if we still possess a lump.
I see no reason to allow them up, do you?
I admit one or two of their claims, of course, but I'll thump
all the rest in Chancery 'ere I sweeten *their* cup.
Yes I know, my dear, 'tis tricky to understand
how they've grown so many, so sudden. To give 'em their due
they have all advanced funds, and hold my Bills at Hand.
They will just have to wait for something to turn delightfully up.

On reading Jennifer Maiden

Jennifer Maiden's first book of verse, Tactics, *was published in 1974. It is a barren waste of words spread like hot and angry pebbles in a merciless sun. It contains not one line of beauty, or even of wistfulness. It is a truly horrible little book, and one has to wonder what strange editorial twist of sadism allowed it to see the light of day. The back cover carries the news that: "In her poetry social irony is often deliberately balanced with lyricism, sensuality and humour....She is interested in the Labor party, and married." One piece in this collection, arguably even more incomprehensible than its awesome mates, is entitled* Haptic Chess, *and purports to deal with a commentary by Herbert Reed [sic] on Henry Moore.*

Mongols are flimsy hands:
ouch! Do not scrimp your pity, but cage
moist fists in a sliver of tusk.
        "I need
a game of Haptic chess, so as to feed
my under-knowledge."
It screams in a hushed hiss like acid spilt on the board.

Your move. Checkmate.
     No. Reverse that, to backwards spin
in a riot of fleeing bishops.
     Does this Queen grow fat on the public purse?
or does she freeze, exhausted, armed?

Or is she plucked and pulled this way and that
by rebellious pawns, who have locked her in?
Has, in fact, her mind run away with her,
and is she abandoned here, by her own men?

Could it be she is not a queen, but a simple maiden
thrust to this terrible prominence, forced to perform?
Told she must sweep the board, and thus heavily laden
gibber her way toward Bethlehem, to be born?

Born Again

A cold brick hall in Perth, and a preacher be-jeweled with pimples
from the tip of his nose to the base of his skinny neck.
Fat jostling girls, confessing their sins, which are no confession at all
but a celebration, rather, that the spotlight has fallen on them.
A sea of enthusiasm, with phosphoro-electric waves
flickering. An eerie bonhomie, as the preacher cheers
us on to hug and kiss and clasp our neighbours fast
as they used to do in the catacombs, when Christ was pure.

Why are they all so ugly, right at this peak of their joy,
with salvation lingering by, and they the pale elect?
And if so hand-picked and chosen, why herd themselves together
in these prim and dingy caves where each reassures the rest?
Faith runs riot here, indeed it lords over all
poor fools like me, whose beliefs are of balsa wood.
Old Luther pounding the table, screeching "Let God be *God*!"
And Erasmus mumbling back: "Nay, let God be good."

Death, yon hooting loon

Death, yon hooting loon, you have chased me down.
Babbled me out of my wits, and confounded me.
Left me grasping at phantoms, and rotten hope.
I loathe thee, Death, and thy worm-eaten mystery,
and detest thy mother, Pain, with whom you'd elope
in a scissor-snip, had you keys from the Town.
Ah, Death, you have conquered me. Small victory, this.
'Tis thy mother who has scored, not thee.
I do not fear your black abyss, but from her
bleak gifts and blandishments I would bug-eyed flee.
In fact, she grips me, whereas you do but wave a blur
upon my future sense, and decaying bliss.

    Thou art a weakling, Death, and a Mother's Boy.
    'Gainst her thou art but foetor, and a grinning toy.

Evensong in Norfolk

Shadows harden in the chapel, as the light shrinks,
and the sun's long, dusty beams dissolve.
Embroidered cushions lie here and there, and books
of Common Praise are idly stacked on the pews.
A verger potters about, or is it the priest
of this fen-lost church of the Norfolk Wash?
The light is too faint to tell, and the silence
utters no secret up to this stranger crew.

We stand in the tiny porch, and innocently peer in.
To Australian minds it is all too quaint and pert.
The stone-flagged nave, and miniature reredos
with its painted parables of gilt and blue.
A tomb or two inside for the local worthies,
and a smell of velvet dipped in honey and dust.
The ornament austere and forbidding.
A building given up to its mossy rust.

Later that night we return for Evensong,
which is held on odd occasions even here.
The crooked old pottering thing we saw before
is the priest, of course, since these hidden glens
have not the resource for Marmelukes.
The organ, though, is cranked by an ancient dame
of some older rite, who has here volunteered
to wreak her petty magic of squeaky hymns.

There are only six to the worship, including us,
and the other four seem edgy that we are here.
The whitened and crumpled priest, unaware of this,
gives his reedy welcome to all who would seek his cheer.
He spreads his arms like a spindly bird, and his thin cry
invokes as a druid's would deep and shivering things:

> *Keep me as the apple of an eye;*
> *Hide me under the shadow of thy wings.*

Elegy for Ezra Pound

*Written upon the occasion of the death of Ezra Pound at the age of 87.
Caratacus (spelt variously) was the British king, or chieftain, defeated by
Claudius in 43 A.D., and betrayed by the Brigantian queen
Cartimandua. He was taken to Rome where he was treated with due
honour, and even pomp, by Claudius Imperator.*

I.

There is such a thin line, my friend
Of fancy: you in some white room,
Me anaesthetised by silence.
A brittle tight-rope wire extends
From Venice to your other shore,
Straining towards infinity.
There is not much can be revived:
Eighty seven years insane.
Pisa gushing into London;
Moist thoughts of a celluloid brain.

II.

These are the streets stripped of matter,
Et vulgus — seething mobs scattering raucous
Orgies of beer and frustration.
The ape, hemmed in with chatter:
No simpleton god slobbered for compensation
This time, Caratacus.

This animal, with fire for beard,
Stamping through dense forests of derision,
A blooded shark amongst minnows.

How he must have spewed under the pines:
Alone, revolted, forgotten Ithaca.
He alone was returning. Angry nannies
Caper their dance of death, surround their
Gums with hissed dribulets of air.

Mania, too, was his excuse.

III.

Il miglior fabbro. You were
and yet were not. Tiny jewels
Glint in perfect exactitude,
Nothing woven from nothing.
You blundered from irregular ages
Clutching a fistful of epigrams,
Creating a subtle kind of disgrace
In the passive fear of the populace.
Lacrimae rerum knew not seems.
I cannot endure such structured screams
Pound, your tortured poems
drift from the twittering twilight pages.

IV.

It is not right, this winding down
Which ends with an exhausted plop,
This free fall into silence.
Your hand lingers, like a leaf,
To establish a reality.
The inky agony of a wretched life
Tumbles towards totality.

Spirit, yesterday I walked where people spat
At incarnate fertility. Enormous trees,
Naked, made me humble. In the heat
Of utter loneliness we licked our sores
To a shunting pattern of half-created light.

You saw
Me debase myself with this endless fiddling
With the over-scoured teats of creativity;

We were
Engrossed in the shredded stumps, the gleaned rewards,
This trickle of sun encircling our infinity.

V.

This hoarding up and disgorging air,
Sometimes talking, others farting;
Caught in the light of some ancient parting,
Curdling silky streams of hair.

It was a waste of breath.

(The savage, they say, remained in Rome,
Tame with the daughter of Claudius;
Almost merged with Penelope,
Yet never forgave his Italy).

It was a feeble death.

A clotted dribble of honey
Ran from his mouth like words
Into hot little streams of songs
That cannot be understood
By silence. He came, and defined
A century of progression.
The breeze twines the leaves
Past hope of comprehension.
Eighty seven drops
Tremble along a wire,
Reflect fragmented beauty
In liquid fire.

No matter how we twist, I cannot end you,
Ezra Pound.
Words, like your rhythms, are buried
Sound for sound.

Anzac Day, 1995

Variations upon a theme by Sidney Keyes

Dedicated to the memory of Keyes, whose beautiful poem "Remember Your Lovers" is printed in the Appendix to this collection. Sidney Keyes was killed at the age of 20 in Tunisia during the Second World War. He had published one volume of exquisite verse. As will be seen by reference to his poem the phrase "drunk with death's unquenchable wisdom" is Keyes', not mine.

Old men, as you loiter in shadows weakly thrown
From the fires still flickering in your dreams, remember your lovers.

When you flew to war, and buttoned up our hopes,
Our shuddering fears, our gratitude and love,
We fought beside you all those terrible years,
Lying rigid in our beds alone, fighting the tears
Which crept like icy pearls down flinching cheeks.
Old men, who have survived us into the cool of peace,
Remember your lovers as hotly now, as then.

When the simple horror of it effervesced,
And struck you dumb as oxen, with lolling tongues,
When shattered limbs and pools of blood had mocked you all
To silent shame and brooding stew, we came
Like wraiths of loveliness from night's thick pall
To gather you like infants to our breast.
Remember how you hungered for us, then.

And now that age comes circling like a vulture,
With curling claws and last, sad squawk of death,
Your memories tangle — you can dimly see yourself
Run shrieking through a rain of murderous lead
Up some forsaken beachhead in a long-forgotten war:
Old men, drunk with death's unquenchable wisdom,
Remember the lovers abandoned on that shore.

And as your memory prods the embers of your thought,
Provoking showers of leaping sparks from dwindling fires,
Do not forget the vows we struck in tenderness
Or that lunge of life that drove our deep desires
Criss-cross beneath your trenches, even as you fought.

Old ones, who feebly hoist salute to fallen men,
Remember your lovers now, as you promised us then.

The Pulse of Poetry

'Tis the pulse what tells of the living; the beat and the throb
of blood through the veins and ventricles — ay, there she lives!
Be it six bars slow and ponderous, or array of fives,
or the lilting Irish beat of the tripping capriped,
or a mystery of dissonance, a riot of vowel
cushioning angry consonants, concepts stood on their head.
But if life beat not sure in the body, then 'tis surely dead.

The Doctor feels at the flickering pulse and claws back a life
that to all intents and purposes has willingly fled.
The words on a page seem bleak and strange, and we clutch at the force
which drives the lines like drumbeats, 'til it seems what is said
is a rat-a-tat-tat of rhythmic wisdom, a cosmic hymn
which drives the brain to a frenzy, and limbs to strife.
But if life beat not sure through the body, then sure, it is dead.

Pompilius Erect

This is rich new sport! They had not mentioned this
when they arranged his marriage. He had thought women
such gabbling, leaky things, beyond both desire and need.
But to thrust like this into them, and unleash his seed!

This Hateful Love

As yet she burns in this my dreamt caress,
shorn of substance, reared it seems from air,
but ever real as all she lovely was
with silken eyes, and angry gypsy hair.

If dreams could lie, so living death might wriggle,
our flesh besot, and rancour cancel all.
What touched and clutched, each pleasure-ridden struggle
bound up to loss, and lost beyond recall.

The image fades. Knowing, we engage,
and mind's a blade to harp such brittle strings;
this hating love spits kisses from its rage
and red with lips of poison, memory stings.

So shred we witless all our guilt of thought
and weft of words wherein our pain is dressed,
but o, how mindless love so sharp has fought
to dream thee thus, and settle in thy breast!

Epitaph for an Engineer

C.Y. O'Connor, perhaps the only prophet
we have suffered, drew up his plans
in a surfeit of imagination;
submitted the grand conception
to his bland companions
for what it was worth.
Blew his brains out, when it transpired
the architect was no longer required.

No fable this, nor fussy public servant
bronzed up for lack of heroes:
for a blind second, silly little Perth
shone central to an epic vision,
thrusting water to the ends of the earth.

Norfolk Bells

bells
in the morning
tumble clinging
bells
bouncing full-blown
singing,
tears into mood and matter
wrangling thus
and bears small infants' swelling
breast and proud stamp
in clad chatter

wrapped bells
in the clear frost
welling
o St Margaret's yelling
boom hoard of bells!

The Poet Grows Old

You are old, and that is all:
Eighty years, and nothing come of it.
Your life a litter of thoughts
half-worked into rhyme,
and a small crop of daughters
who trick out your remaining time
with circumstantial pomp. Nothing more.

Once, it appears, there could have been a girl,
for a dim shadow haunts your modest verse,
a simpering voice muffled beyond a private,
mildly menacing door.
But now even memory lies
like a slug in the morning frost,
stiff and sore. You smoke, and mumble happily.
Nothing moves the vacuum of your eyes
except Death's caress, with her scrabbling claw.

In Spandau

for John Harper-Nelson, one of Hess' British guards at Spandau

I sit in Spandau prison, turning my helicopter hat
about and about on my head, an unending curl.
The guards rotate like seasons. British, Russians, French.
Their faces come and go like leaves in autumn.
I am punished here. The rest have crisped, and fallen,
Doenitz, Speer, the others. Dead, released, forgotten.
Just I, Rudolph, remain, dark dregs in a drunken bottle.

We had good talk here. Our dream was all undone,
but with years to spare we wove it all anew.
We were crabby with each other. Doenitz never would
accept what happened, what spike had thrust us through.
I could. So could Speer. After all, in here,
the inevitable suppurates through every little pore.
I sit, and revolve my hat, and gaze at lowering walls.

I will die here, in my box. That thought does not appal
me as it used. They have built my coffin early.
I am told we killed millions, Speer says uselessly.
He wanted them for labour. That makes sense.
You should not lock Germans in, they will bunch up,
wait 'til the Rhine is frozen, and pour across.
We are a vicious race, though kind to our kin.

I was never fond of Hitler, but we needed him
as the Mongols needed Ghengis Khan. When nations burst
they need at their head some mannequin. He was
the dullest fellow really, weedily thin,
a cartoon cutout cut-throat, indecisive, aloof.
We deserved no better. I suppose he was mad,
as we all were: crazily eager, hot at the hoof.

We enjoyed our hats, and uniforms. And our rank seemed so mighty
for middling folk. Goering, of course, expected it.
But Goebbels — what in God's name would he have done
in an ordinary world, what would he have become?
And Himmler — where would he fit in? I think, in an asylum
where he would be bully nurse with his horrid spectacles
and pudgy little gills. Yes, that is where he would have swum.

We writ large what has ever been, and that which will come.
Cruel we were, and wasters of power, as politicians are.
Our bunting is faded and torn, and we left millions dead
in our murderous wake, and millions more forlorn.
For which they punish me, legions of the dust,
and hem old Rudolph here, like a cockroach in a box.
I accept the verdict. Crass, barbaric, but just.

I wish Albert still were here. Philosophical, he was.
He gave me comfort that we were not all dross.
How he came to hate us all! Yet he was with us
'til the end, and should thereby help heave at our cross.
The others shot or poisoned themselves. A quick escape
from their nothingness to an even greater void.
A sharp crack to their brain, then a white emptiness.

The guards peer through my lattice, midwife to my dreams,
but irritable chore to them. How they must resent
this endless watching of a tired and sick old man.
They watch me twist my hat round and round on my head
and conclude that I am mad, as I have ever been.
I am the last of the Reich that was to last a thousand years.
Its relic, rather. My hat turns tight upon a million screams.

Pelican Point

They bob and duck in water, like fusspot wives,
and ribble their feathers with sticky beaks, as if for fleas.
Others float serene, trying to look like swans,
although gawkish, fiddly ones. In the salty breeze
which comes loitering over Crawley they fluff themselves
like aldermen, their eyes beady, and keen.

Out on the spar of sand that is Pelican Point
sits a rumpled youth, in a flair of embroidered jeans.
His shirt is loose and thin, and his tangle of hair
is bedecked with beads, and flecks of silvereens.
A girl, too, is there, aloof and disjoint
as she squints at the waddling birds, and aslant at him.

They have come to pick at their lunch, as have the birds,
to let sunshine's fingers gild these whispering waves.
Alone in this tiny fellowship, just specks
in this wildering waste of sand, and hollowing caves.
They roll in the shallows like wrecks, with bubbles of words
looping up to the surface, where they softly spit.

A pelican shudders its wings, and suddenly soars
in a bursting fury of water into fearful flight.
The girl gives a start of terror, and the distant boy
tenses briefly, as if the shadow of night
had brushed with ink the sun's white pores.
A chill clings to the heat's remorseless tremor,

as the great birds shuffle, and settle to fishing once more.
There is majesty in the awkwardness of their gait
and an ooze of belonging plashing about their shore.
To Pelican Point flock the underweight, and the sad.
The city a myth in the distance, humming late
through the crumbling afternoon, like a crooning hag.

Galope Muerto

This is a very loose translation — more of a transliteration, really — of Pablo Neruda's great poem of the same name. Some of the images are Neruda's, some are mine, but one is borrowed directly from W.H. Auden's lines:

> We were to trust our instincts, and they came
> Like corrupt clergymen filthy from their holes.

I have tried to capture some of the dense richness to be found in Neruda's work and, indeed, that of the Spanish poets generally, meaning that this poem is more a translation of style than of meaning.

Like ashes strewn thick through peopled seas
swirl the shadows of this slow dusk.
From a pueblo of pin-prick lights, bells are foaming
softly, lapping at this harbour where the roads criss and cross.
Sound is teased from the metal, rung like a gong
of summoning, fast fused in the dust
of distance, and night's deep hymn. Lithe shapes harden:
things remembered, and things barely seen
if seen at all, like figs dropped, forgotten in the garden,
pashed with noiseless, idle fingers, rotting green.

Ah, but it is swift, this lunge of living,
rattling endless, as a madly dangling pulley
sizzled wild with rope forever spins.
Great trees stitch it with their tossing
limbs of needle, a canyon hugely full
of night's weird rustle, an ocean flecked with fins.
Ah, but rough it is, this storm of living,
squalls of a sudden, though the wind were scarcely whispering
through the nodding murmur of lilies at the convent's sealed door;
or death's surge of blood to the bull's lolling tongue,
snipped in a terrible shudder, plunged in the tumble
of his yelling head, shriek of his horns struck dumb.

Which twists and picks me, like a lover's feeblest cries,
like a breath of feathers fluttering above;
like a bee's death, like an alphabet —
ay, everything my pallid heart will neither fathom
nor embrace, tears which glister in a hungry eye,

men's endless struggle, and their whirling wars,
dirty acts come fumbling out like clergymen
from weedy dens, the shouldering ice which climbs and claws
in a vast, disordered ocean — ay, for me, pale troubadour,
with my song's buckler, and my toy sword.

So tell me then why I hear this soft surge of doves
and what bears them gentle between night and time?
Or that tremble of bells, floating like rain
from the darkness, sprinkling jewels of thin wine.
This flicker of an hour, the night a sparkle of beauty,
stretched out of mottled time to eternity.

Reared along the cliffs, in an amulet of summer dusk,
the calabash trees are looped with listening.
The bells twist in their branches. They are without blame, or pity,
grown rich with weather, yet neither accepting nor giving
from their stature. I weave in their tilting shadows
to stroke their stillness, feeling here and here
for their fullness, laden with heavy drops.

Felix Rotund

for Cookie

This cat is huger than a football
and glares with happy rage.

She will soon thrust her kin upon us.

Their Spanish Thing

for Pete and Marg, mis compañeros de viaje

First they wintered in Valencia, where the orange groves
lie thick as gold in a pirates' hoard, in endless gleam.
Young and irresponsible, foolishly rich and loose,
Spain their make-believe kingdom — they wore it on their sleeves
of quilted cloth, and fine down. They dawdled in the sun
which cast its soft heat willy-nilly, not just on them,
but on all the slouching cavalcade of their foreign dream.
They sank into wine like sponges soaking up blood.

And south, to Andalusia, white cottages and huts
spread out like a feast of bitty items, strung along hills,
guitars in the dry night air, crescent moon above
like a scimitar, tall palms murmuring in hot repose.
Toothless gypsies grinning at them, and mincing sluts
winking and beckoning, at least to him. Clumps of daffodils
in sun-caked dirt, here and there a sweating rose
like jewels set in concrete, small isotopes of love.

Then back to Cataluña, to the savage surge of the Ebro
through Miravet de Ebro, where it snakes towards Tortosa.
Where peasants plod in history's haze, and the castle soars
like a falcon rampant, high on its thyme and rosemary hill.
Miravet, near Mora. In his mud and concrete tavern old Amadeo
serves up his *Calisay* in tiny dollops, with tremulous skill.
Old men dicker at cards. His daughter, dappled with *sonrisa,*
bustles fat with her brooms and mops, as if they were oars.

They sit *al fresco*, as they call it, soaking up the sun,
whilst life hustles about them, eager to eat and bed.
They are treated kindly. They are from beyond the circle of hills
which defines the *ribera*, and thereby welcomed, as welcomes run.
Their money here is worthless, for a single peseta fulfils
most business bargains, and a tab is kept for the rest.
They are unusual here, impervious, *inglés*,
and their blundering understanding leaves nothing to be said.

They are taught some scraps of Catalan. This to impress
their new-found friends, who in turn are impressed by Australian.
Like desert tribes' strange meetings, odd mouthings float
twixt stranger folk, as native speaks to alien.
Under the Spanish sun, hands clasp in a simple hosannah
of earthy joy — ah, to be alive! To dress
in weird garb and silly hat, to dance the *Sardana*
in an all-inclusive ring, to leap and cavort like a goat!

That was their Spanish thing. They will not quick forget
those nights of dark azure, the sleaze of the *Plaza Real*
in bustling Barcelona, with gypsy thieves askew,
nor their village in the hinterland, sleepy Miravet,
nor Amadeo waddling round his tables and his trees,
nor the crumbling cheesecake castle, nor friends they made withal,
nor the wine they drank, nor the bread they brake, nor the feasts
        of olive and cheese
they made there, and left littered there, as they stumbled through.

Pompilius Alone

It is time now, my little life is done,
I feel the poison in me lurch and wheeze.
I cart my body about, a laden automaton.
My liver, says my doctor, thick with disease.

There is nothing I have essayed which will last
with more impression than a mountain breeze;
nothing I have loved, or loving, lost,
to monument my useless life, or to tease

a tender memory later in some other's mind.
I have watched my days drop legion like the autumn leaves
to swirl away in the wind. O, if there is one who grieves
for wasted lives, remember Pompilius! (If you'd be so kind).

Ode to the Confounded Dead

*Written in 1976 upon the occasion of the Author achieving the
distinction of graduation from the University of Western Australia as a
confirmed Bachelor of literature.*

Farewell, you tillers of my youth,
studied cares, and learned cell,
pedlars of the tattered Truth
and scrimping scholars all, farewell.

Demetrion, so bloated fat,
with yellow eyes that gleam despair,
the aspect of Jehosophat
sits grinning in this rancid bear,

whilst at his back, subordinates
inspect their fear, click their knives;
such putrid hugeness titillates
the razor hopes of little lives.

As he rumbles, Chaucer, Langland,
sweep in soaring, booming sound:
until he burps. On every hand
his snoring students hedge him round.

And look who darts, with lists of books
emblazoned round his shrivelled frame,
with sharpened eyes, and frightened looks,
and unrequited love of fame:

why, little *Beady*! Patrick White's
most energetic *translateur*,
who creaks with joy to fuse delights
and melt them in an ashen blur;

and scribbles essays, which become
his want of children, darling boys,
with shrieks of spleen if anyone
should dare to meddle with his toys.

Listless wives, men of inaction,
pale young women like frightened deer,
angry nuns erect from fiction
and witless actors moulder here.

And all the rest sequestered lie
in one another's sorrow bled,
suckle their pain, struggle to die,
endlessly lecture, babble and bed.

Poets who have scraped the soul
and coaxed a voice to wildly sing
are neatly plastered to the Whole
and Sensitised to Everything.

Sound is scattered in the sense,
and beauty flattened into forms,
as each dense student struggles hence
besmeared with intellectual norms.

Little pods of lacquered learning
shrink and blister in the sun.
You have squandered everything
to gain your pew in Babylon.

At every soul you tempt and kill,
at blistering each racing heart,
at each such conquest you fulfil
your ragged dreams as whores of art.

And o, the self-inspecting woe
which struggles from your drooping lips,
as endless meanings come and go,
and scissor-minded age clips.

Withered lives in dripping iron,
scorching armour, strips you bare.
You are undone by your profession,
reft of joy, immured there.

So fare thee well, my pride of youth,
huddled care, and barren cell;
warders of your desperate truth
and fading scholars all, farewell.

Footsteps

Spain, 1978

Where are they going
in the gaudy night,
in the pea-green light
of Barcelona?

And why do they stumble
briefly thus, and teeter,
like the sharp, quick clatter
of the dice, rattled by street kids
huddled in wide-eyed concert
in the *Plaza Real*?
Stutter, then recover,
mumbling along, drunkenly spritely,
swung on a pillar
tipsily up, luck likely.

o where then are they slewing
like hell-defying hymns,
hauled up what bright ladders?
or green in the darkness slithering
loose, liquid limbs
down what lick-lipping adders?

The Wealth of Nations

Written in 1977 upon the occasion of the Author having negotiated a successful wager with Messrs Ladbrokes of London, the sagacity of which lay in the successful prediction of the outcome of a game of English football, in which sport the happy (though hitherto penurious) winner had then, and has now, no interest whatsoever.

Ah, this thick slab of five pound notes,
fat concubine of trivial pleasure;
you secure my future for another month
and underwrite my leisure.

All so fresh and innocent:
there is carte-blanche for anything you do.
Doors clipped in the beggar's face
spring open for you.

Yes, you are welcome everywhere. But the price is high,
and commerce takes its toll.
For when you have reaped your full return
of human hope and happiness,
slipped through the hands of prudent men
to wild, more desperate lovers,
you — the agent of our concern,
bright broker of life's disturbing bargain,
you will have *nothing* to call your own,
no, not one small commemorative item,

save, perhaps, the certain knowledge
and rueful idiot's end of immolation
in the holocaust of millions,
bound in thick packs to well-worn others,
pitchforked filthy and wrinkled
into hell's hot mouth,
without sensation.

Our seed is scattered
and we with it.
See where crimson sperm
trickles in the firmament:
see there, see there!

For this gift, these secrets,
I was guaranteed creation.

I remember charging, the pack of us,
streaming our pain, storming the well-kept villas;
things land-locked in memory.
I remember. We were drunk,
run to seed on paeans of jubilation.
we were young and foolish, our poison
was that promise of perfection:
or not poison, we were beside ourselves,
for a moment understood
all our throbbing desire
before the pain bolt ripped us,
before the fire.

People scudding, cities of rust and torpor:
I have lived too long, I have lived too long.
My frail body fidgets, and vapours away.
Et exspecto mortuorum resurrectionem.
My blood pitches and tosses at remembering perversity.
All our wearisome losses are dwindled blobs of memory.

Leve moder, your daughter-son
crawls through caverns of calloused flesh:
        leet me in.
Leve moder, you burgeon at one
with your fructive future, divine vagina
        leet me in.
Bearing the cycle of crucifixion,
burial and restitution,
        leet me in, o leet me in.

Can I seek forgiveness
for creation squandered?
I cannot brick in the pictures
whence my thoughts have wandered.
There is no one to guide me,
there is poverty in memory.
My loins pucker and seethe,
my tortured body is offered;
I have not fed of the flesh,
but was wild in my youth,
and have suffered.

It was not you deserted me
my fondling emulsion;
Close in upon me, my story,
cloak my oblivion.

I had my gods, my reasons
which slipped from grace;
I wilt and surge with the seasons
tormenting my disgrace.

This memory flickers now, and flings
crazed rhythms at the senses,
not rag-time reminiscences
but deep textured things:

I feel the heaving godhead flow
through rotten bones, I brush that face,
that blast of liquid lightning know,
and suffocate in that embrace.

At C.A.T.S.

I worked briefly at a children's theatre group in Perth (C.A.T.S.) in the 1970's. An old derelict had taken up virtual residence out the back, much to the chagrin of one of the arts bureaucrats attached to the institution.

I.

A queer relic, this discarded fossil
of a man, mouldy and unwholesome.
He slumps all bundled in the sun
reeking of drink and sinking years,
hiccoughing puddles of laughter,
saliva spread with his thick-witted thumb.
Wine glistens in the harvest of his cheek
and his chewed lips dangle
like a lewd zip undone.
He often strolls unsteadily in
to check our work with his weird advice
and slurred reminiscence.
Bemused by human industry
he can still cull a trick or two
from his battered sieve of memory
long punctured through.
He drinks a gallon of port a day,
babbles away to his radio
with a voice all slaked and spent;
full of his insignificance,
and his weak content.

II.

This other one, of some small importance,
tumbles into my office self-impressed.
"We shall have to do something about the situation,
you know, it will have to be addressed."
He heaps his hopeful cares in a tangle
of awkward thought extruded from desire;

half stretches to caress,
but prudent as he is,
is quick to suppress,
and as quick to retire.

He is keen to ensure his permanence
with his firm grip upon order;
stamping his footprints in the blank expanse
of the world's water.

Incredibly Long Haiku

*An observation upon a poetry reading at the Perth Artists Club. One
more bloody syllable, and we'd have six full Haiku here!*

The Poet rises. Hush descends.
Red lips arch like a bent bow.
We await the arrow's lethal dart.

It is a poem of Himself.
It is lengthy.
He is lonely, and depressed.

The string twangs noisily
along its shaft;
the target audience shuffles,
puzzled and unimpressed.

Memory sucked and plucked
until teased apart.
Nobody takes much notice
of such tense art.

A guilty silence. The clink of a cup.

Nobody cries, or hunches up.

Nobody laughs.

Shakespeare, to his daughter aged ten

for Chay Moran

What — art ten now? Presumptuous miss, thou art dame
in my household, mistress of all which can laugh and sing.
Thou hast pinched the keys of thy mother — in her sweet name
thou hast stripped our kingdom, robbed us of everything!

You must not age, my darling. Just nestle here,
lest the world in losing thee should dull its hue,
and, growing old, you cheat it of its treasure
as Winter frosts the Spring's delicious dew.

No, ten is old. So old it seems eternity
since bud first burst from these poor withered boughs;
I would I could live ten times ten years only
and live each ten as rich as we have ours.

For then, my love, I'd dwell amongst the fairies
and no hobgoblin fear could flush me out,
nor toothless witch, nor bawling troll would scare me
from the magic spell which gossamers our house.

And ten times ten we'd wander in our forests,
a hundred times hunt shells along the beach,
hear wind stir up the cries of mermaid ghosts
and shiver at their singing, each to each.

And never, growing stiff, would we be bidden
to the stingy feast doled out to elder folk:
No rent, no toil, nothing to be hidden
in the grubbiness of shame, or ruined hope.

No. Ten is old — 'tis ancient, e'en — 'tis commonsense.
Dost think thy father wise for being forty?
He hath forgotten all of any consequence.
'Tis *wicked* to be old, else it's stupid. Nay. 'Tis naughty.

Hu Ic Geswincdagum

'Hu ic geswincdagum' comes from the third line of the great Anglo Saxon poem The Seafarer, *translated in the standard edition as "How I, in toilsome days..."   I think the glorious phonetic word 'geswincdagum' deserves something better than this. Whether my own "How I, in youth's mad maelstrom..." approaches this I shall leave for the reader to judge.*

How I, in toilsome days, made light of weather
foul on my sea-cheek, and turned to water's wearing;
With youth wasted, and time turning, like the tide.
Cannier than merchant now, grizzled with getting,
hugged into house, with wealth's thick oilskin bearing
'gainst wave and dashing foam, snug in my pride.

It seems but yesteryear we ran stout ship into froth,
timber tilted, mast tall as towering tree;
Heaved her into water, laughed as she rolled
and righted, leapt in, and roped her through
the showering surf: ai, how she swathed sheer
in the shimmering sapphire crush, and shot free!

So young, and foolish, in our supple ships,
lust enlivened, full of booty's dream.
Gold to greedy gorge, maidens shrieking as they fled
and monkish muddlers we might catch, and spit.
Ah, old whimpering men to turn above the coals like pigs!
And the girls, squelched wet with fear, to drag to bed.

I shudder to remember it. Honour grew cold
and stark as sharpened steel on such wild trips.
What little plunder we could harvest from the peasants
in their hovels was so thinly spread amongst us
I can scarce remember one full hold
we homewards hauled, bold pirates, slaked with slaughter.

I see them now come gathering, about the village,
as ice unravels winter's thrall, young wolves let loose
to sniff the sea, and smell her salty mud;
to dream of world-rule from the prow of a ship
let loose on the seas by them, and their bawling brood
of brotherhood, and their bond of murderous blood.

They buy of me, the old chandler, rope for their ships,
and pitch to caulk them thick through squall's great toss.
They laugh as I dodder about my shop to serve their wants
and fain would plunge into plunder 'ere pillage has begun.
Save a few, who remember Aelfric, or have heard of my trips
across the wide wave wilderness, when I was young.

Hu ic geswincdagum, how I in youth's mad maelstrom
led them futurely to this, and bred them to kill.
I nuzzle my wife in her garden, and squeeze her behind
with a hand which has splintered skulls with a blow of an axe.
The ships set sail from our fjord; I can hear dim cries
of contempt and joy, as they wave to me on my hill.

Devine Cliches

*in which the Author was challenged by Mr Frank Devine, of The
Australian newspaper, to a cliche-creation competition, designed by
the latter worthy to rescue the language from the blight of the
commonplace, and to assist the suppression of good ol' sayings.*

I'd rather go searching midst haystacks for needles
then hunt out a foil in a forest of tin,
or search out a man midst the whines and the wheedles
down Oxford Street's mincing play-acting of sin;

A blessing disguised is but penance in motley,
'twere better by half to cloak pleasure with guilt;
I would rather the vicar made heaven's sign sweetly
than see it wrapped up in pain's tawdry quilt.

In short, I'll leave not a pebble unturned,
not a furrow unploughed, nor a can left its lid,
not a blonde left unravished, nor redhead unburned
until I've made match of my Ego and Id.

Like a bat out of hell I'll make scorn of my fury,
and eyeless in Gaza, will peer at myself;
the eyes of the soul my judge and my jury,
while the moth doth corrupt, and rust eat my wealth.

I'm aware that such verse is unpopular stuff,
ripe with the sweetness and squalor of vice,
my metaphors tired, and ancient enough,
my similes scattered, and imprecise,

But I'd rather the sun still slip over the arm
before hitting the booze; that boys remain boys;
that girls still smell sweetly of sugar and balm
and men still be led by Napoleon's toys;

That the home fires still sparkle up chimneys of love,
and that soldiers might feel there was point to their strife;
that God should sit bearded, pouting above,
that a man might discover he's in love with his wife,

And that all of the wisdom we have passed through the press
might be bottled and quaffed 'til we've seen off the hearse,
by those who simplicity still can impress
with cantation of prayer, and the cliches of verse.

Shakespeare (old) to Anne Hathwey

Thou tell'st me that thou *love'st* me, old daggletail? Love such a
fool? Ay, even the fool must be loved, lest he turn to clown. For the
clown is the fool's fool, he is what poor fools become. And rich
fools? Ah, they turn to warriors, playwrights and kings; they strut
and fret for a moment in life's brief splendour; they argue and
bicker, they fight, lose and win; and in all of these things, and all
their strivings, they long to be loved. On this deep desire is based all
of their sorrow, and on this feeble hope they are lifted on wings. So
to tell me that you *love* me — 'tis sacred that, such simple spell.

All the verses I have writ, all the turmoil, all the strife, all the
passion, all the grief, all the fervour, all the wit: wind it into one
thick ball and hurl it spinning far from hence; let all I've done make
one thin wall around this tangled skein of sense: *I — love — you.*

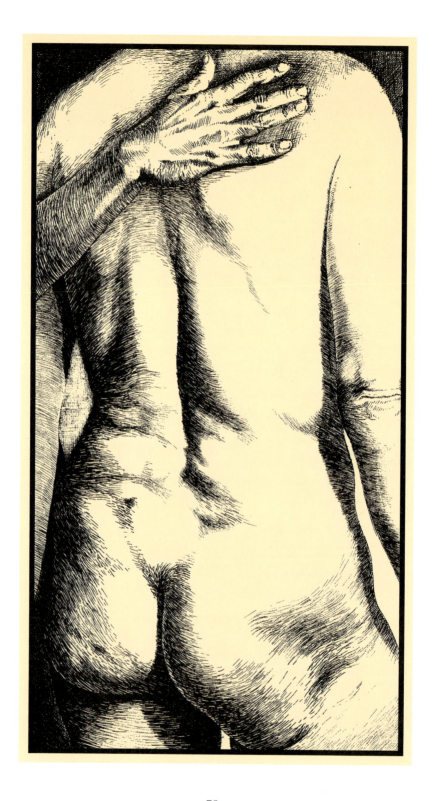

78

The Luck of the Draw

For Marg Merrilees

London, 1939 — Clive and Bunty are to be married at last, to the delight
of society, which had despaired of them.

The luck of the draw, that's what it is:
Clive and Bunty, hoist on high
in the crisp gloss of this week's romance,
a-squirm with pride, and in public view,
what's more, the delight of millions.
Or so it seems to them. They are in love.

War flickers in the wings
and the dread Bosch
seem everywhere;
lump lovers into ovens
along with the others
hot and bare.

They select a flat in Kensington,
unaware of danger,
or snot-nosed doodlebugs
flopping from the sky.
Cupboard space is important
in their bunker, but in short supply.
Was that the whisker of a finger
frisking my new silk dress?
Do the draughts rustle my vestments
thus? Have I managed to impress?

She has her innocent wiles
carefully sprung
with wide-eyed fear
and dreams of men.
He, like a toy volcano,
erupts when depressed,
all but blotting out the sun.

Such a precious plaything
counsels caution,
and the prize exhibit
(i.e. Clive)
is o so jealously won.

My wet shank and livid lip
are yours for the barter:
ask for me, I shall come!
Passed underfoot by crunching columns
we shall grovel each in other
for an instant, for one black night
in the foul bilge of the trenches,
and with love's lewd carcase slung on our hip
stagger spent to the slaughter.

Thus may we fuse in unison
with marriage as our end.
Always the thieves of love,
unusually rank and ugly,
angrily contend.
And always the kind, unbearable soul
who advises, bending with care to listen,
and is just a friend.

Every shrew shall be tamed
in law, and Love thrill lips to move
with decent fire:
Clive and Bunty shall be married!
Bells hover, anxious, proud to prove
the meek rout of unprincipled desire.

Cradled in this stiff claw
they read for company alone,
however poor. Or perhaps it is safer
in hyperbole, beyond the door
of fact and fantasy's fierce glow,
this pig-hunt, this all-consuming war.

Sleeping at Yanchep, 1995

for Rod Moran

Light the fire, Rod, and leave me here to sit
in a wonderland of dreams, and thoughts that flicker back;
Let me settle in your couch, and dull my slippery wits
with wine from your cardboard barrel, and a jumble of snack.

You're poor, you claim. As auditor and businessman
I prowl about your asset-hoard to gauge your wealth;
The works of art upon your wall are gifts of love
and bear no price. The shelves bulge with books, as the earth

heaves with flowers and shrubs, but these will not fetch
any value at auction. Your things are hard to impress
on the scale of values. You seem to regard a poem or sketch
from a friend more highly than a contract. We must also assess

your wife, with her golden waterfall of riotous hair,
and your beautiful pixie daughter, who will break the hearts of men
when she blossoms. I doubt you are even half aware
of these treasures at your fingertips, or of what you earn from them.

Outside, the sky is layered up with pink and grey,
your tame old crow taps beak on stone, and vents his wheeze;
slender gums, like delicate women, sigh and sway
in the soft embrace of the ocean's slithering breeze,

which has shaken out a velvet blanket over me
as a sluggish swooning creeps through weary limbs;
in this humble temple-dwelling of philosophy
I am lulled to sleep by centuries of hymns;

As at this altar, grim and proud, are gathered
all who have fought for decency, and truth, and art;
Their works inspire this household, which is lathered
thick with learning, love and cunning craft;

And this in turn breathes pleasure's breath through all you do:
your tiny family squabbles, thin, and shorn of vice,
your poverty, your pride. It has been carved by you
this place of peace, this artefact, this paradise.

Lizardry

Today I crushed a lizard on my patio,
just wandering there. I'd thought myself alone
in time's small space, a-squandering
the sun's rich shower as it drenched
these flaky timbers with its golden guile.

No doubt he felt secure there, since warmth
so cruelly flatters fear, and melts its stealth.

His intricate belly is spread on the boards
like fish paste on a hunk of bread;
His tail is curved in a sudden rush of pain
and tiny entrails twine his scattered limbs.
And what are these, plucked off: entreating hands,
or fingery legs? Not quick enough of scamper
to flee old flatfoot here, nor deft enough
to oil into crack and crevice, and avoid such crush.

His head is gone — stuck, I expect, to the heels
which ground this fragile life to shreds
in aimless potter from geranium to geranium.

So lizards die, and ants march up to chew
this glorious feast erupted on my patio.
I would give them sugar, honey, or anything
from my cupboard-hoard to swap this life again;
watch him slither off, that tail weave and flick;
I would feed the world such sweetness it would gorge delight
and dizzy it with charity, if one such cunning trick
could pluck alive this churn of silver blue
from the heavy, crunching underfoot
of my remorseless shoe.

Mr Wentworth, squatter, goes a-wooing

Will you come out with me, my black-eyed lass,
down to the thick flowing river, will you step out with me?
I have decked me out in my shiny suit, and my velvet hat
and have brought thee a sprig of violets, and rosemary.

I have little done, and little hope to do,
and have not the cast nor the fire to re-write history.
I must set my hopes around minuscule things, and hope that you
can be stirred by the tiny passions of the likes of me.

A horse I can sit like a king, and can manage men,
and my acres stretch the horizons, as far as the eye can see.
There's books I have carefully read have lent me acumen
and knowledge of life, and its shimmering mystery.

But I cannot mix it with your Sydney wits, or the gents
you host and party — these are fluffy tarts to me.
Speech cut rough from my squatter's tongue, coarse and intense,
makes 'em titter down their saucers, as they slurp their tea.

You must like their merry chatter — indeed, you sit
in the midst of it all like a Queen at court on her soft divan,
marshalling all this chatter, and dragooning it
to your bodyguard of praise. Perhaps you plan

to yield to this siege of weaklings, and permit the rout
of all that is young and that shivers with joy and healthy lust.
Maybe you'd rather sit simpering thus, as the fire burns out
and these wretched simpletons gossip. Perhaps you must

engage them so, and egg them on to their feats
of bitchy hatred, spittly spite, and gleeful spleen.
They are full of the news of Sydney, and from their wrinkled teats
runs the thin black milk of the City, sour and mean.

But I could not shine in this, even if I
were privy to the petty feuds of their circus fare.
My cattle keep me busy, and the sheep-run and sty
blot up what politics I have to spare.

I would have thee, black-eyes, right here on my farm
in the golden west, far from Sydney's clever men.
I have naught else to offer, save that no harm
will be suffered close to thee, in this regimen.

And I am honest, I think, however dull,
and will fulfil thee, as would a horde of faithful slaves.
God knows, I'll serve thy creamy loins, 'til they are full
and graft on them the fruit your tree-stem craves.

And all that I have will be given up to thee,
and you shall become the Empress of my spiky fief.
My wealth shall be yours to spend, for it means nothing to me
'gainst this venture. Indeed, you shall be thief

of all my pennies and pounds, my leisure and life,
and all I had held to be private, and a thing of my own resource.
Yours shall be my pleasure, and to my darling wife
I shall yield as to a meandering watercourse

which picks its banks and curve and cunning twist
with a logic all its own, unstoppable by men.
I cannot chatter sweetly, like a wit or journalist
or other Sydney types of speckled hen;

I cannot talk of Paris, or the salons there,
nor read you subtle poems, writ to the bulging moon.
I cannot woo thee cleverly, nor hope to compare
with these toothy fellows who can make thee swoop and swoon

with the cut and cause with which they are involved,
and their heady talk and their rich philosophy.
I have but copper coin to lay against their gold,
and they would laugh to think they compete with types like me.

But that they do, and I am their enemy
for to me they are weeds that will choke the thing that I love.
I would pluck them up in my fist, if you would tolerate me,
and, godlike, fling them angry from above.

So will you come out with me, my black-eyed girl,
and walk awhile with me beneath the murmuring gums?
Will you hold my eager hand in yours, and let swirl
in your veins the hot red wine of the reckless young?

Will you kiss me with shivering lips, as you used to kiss,
and clutch this poor lump of clay as if to fashion it?
Will you wrench me away from myself, and in ecstasy of this
obliterate all fashion, style and wit?

And in this wilderness of sand and streaky star,
out upon this heath, beneath this southern sky,
will you give yourself to me, and leave thyself ajar
to my stealthy entry, and my lunging cry?

Wongan Hills, Sunday

Cars crawling to service, limp with the heat,
the dull thump of stares. Feeling the leaning,
swatting, wryly wincing bodies drinking
rather sullenly, in the itch of wheat.

They serve no god. Each year they cut and sow
as days patter around them. Their wives drive
and are handy. They come only to know
which winter's ebb has stranded them alive.

Harvest-hoisted, rigged to season,
reaping fancy in female homes;
the seed heaves within the reason
as each speculative eye roams.

The stem palls. There is a growing rhythm of scorn
which scarifies old pasture. The ground yields
shiftless to each new rape. In hostile fields
a boy brazen with summer's fire splashes in corn.

Tawny Port

*Henry Lawson, in that sort of supreme irony reserved for acts of
politicians and bureaucrats, adorned until recently our $10 note.
A poet of great stature, he died a penniless drunk. R.I.P., thou goliard.*

He slouches on the old stone bench, and sips his watery rum
on the lichen-sodden concrete up Victoria down the Cross.
He absorbs the sidelong glances of the street's inveterate dancers
stepping light and high above him, and his reeking air of loss.

Don't mind if I do, boy, that's a decent drop of yours,
if beer counts as drink where you are from. No whisky, sport?
No. Too late, too dark, too wet and damp. See these old claws?
They've scratched some tragic verse up in their time. Got any port?

'Course not! In storm, no port. You shouldn't be here, kid,
so ..... spick, and span. 'Tis naughty night to swim in, oi?
We moths spread whisker wings on oily water, like Gordon did,
'though did him little good. The gutter sucked him in, the silly boy.

Look. Watch the men of Sydney town trudge grimly to and fro
on an endless trek to nowhere, each plodding where he ought;
luckier than most men, yet luckless still they go,
whilst I slump here, watch them pass, and dream of drinking port.

A port, a tawny port! God, I'd kill a man for less!
My tongue slips out for slurp of that, its last sad flopping thought.
A tiny drop of rich man's brew, old Lisbon's soft caress
My birth, my right, take all I've got, for one small glass of port!

I can sense the deep unhappiness which lies upon this town;
I can hear the glum procession of the endless tramping feet;
I can touch the crumbling balustrades, and feel them flaking down,
and the faces melt in misery as I peer along the street.

These are people without history. Sure, they jaw about the bush
and their billies and their campfires, and the Murrumbidgee men,
but the thin black folk they swept aside will infiltrate their push
and yellow eyes glaze greedy on the land they wrenched from them.

And all around this white man's turd flock flies, a million fold,
Malaya, Indonesia, China, Thais and Polynee,
D'ye think they'll leave to Redneck Bill this tranch of fruit and gold
and allow these greedy squatter-folk free will of destiny?

'Course not! Sorry, boy, squeeze down that bench. Pissed me pants
as like as not, or spilt your beer. It's grim, tonight. Those clouds
aswart the moon are black with tears. Our *critics,* idle sycophants,
are on the prowl tonight to blot us out, and spin us shrouds.

This wind glides like a finger down my cheek, sad stubbly thing,
poor breeze so prickled, comfort patched to cheer. You're quiet, lad,
I think you're maybe mournful. Don't these drains stink! Let's sing
of all we might have done, or what *you'll* be, what's been and had!

Phharg! Now, look at that. A jewel of redemption, glob of spit.
T'was part of me, that spectrum, now it's dead. *Alors, c'est ca.*
Moist bloodspots in the desert sands, red rubies caked in shit
are your poems and your paintings and your songs, Australia,

and I hate the growling bitch on heat which shuddered to give birth
to this tangled, mangled nightmare race of bug-eyed, listless men,
gross and fat and beer-drenched, destroyers of the earth,
mindless in your conquering, and mindless now as then!

Shift along the bench, boy. Make way for one small ruin
more to crumble in the dust. I'm sorry if I scared you.
Blame old Henry Lawson, poet, drunkard — a pot to spew in
when you're tipsy and disconsolate, down Woolloomooloo

up Potts Point way, along the Cross, or maze of Darlinghurst,
you'll find him tucked away there, like a crow beneath its hedge;
though rain drip in, and bramble scratch, and lung choke fit to burst
he'll be croaking out his ditties on the city's twilight edge,

where Herrick softly whispers like the rushes in the fens,
where gum trees droop above his head, and magpies still cavort,
where Rabbie Burns still dances in his magic Highland glens
and a table's set for poets, with a wee small glass of port.

The Don Enters In Upon His Own

for John Harper-Nelson

*Written and recited upon the occasion of the wedding of my mother
Helen, to John Harper-Nelson in April, 1993, both of them in the
dotage of their seventies, and both completely mad. Sandy Lewis is a
politician, family friend, and great drinker (until reformed by his wife).*

So yer marryin' me mother — Gawd blimey, but you're game!
She's fifty if a day, and she hasn't any money.
Pretty quick of temper, too, impossible to tame:
She won't wash up, nor darn your socks, and never cleans the dunny.
You might think you snared a goldfinch with your wicked little dart,
But in fact you've shot an albatross directly through the heart.

I s'pose she's good for some things — look at *me*, for one.
If *" by their fruits ye'll know them"*, the lady's pure class.
She's pretty flash at dinner and she likes her bit of fun,
Can drink with Sandy Lewis, and match him glass for glass.
Other skills are travel, dining out and spending money;
Jewels and clothes her pet delights, and living where it's sunny.

So yer marryin' me mother! I'll just pour another gin.
You think you've seen the lot with all your years in the army.
The siege was long, the walls were stout, but now they've folded in
You get to storm the citadel. *We* all think you're barmy.
Not that we're unhappy — we were wondering what to do
with an escalating problem, now resolved in you.

As the Elder of the family I'm supposed to check your means;
Have you round to dinner, try and organise a job.
Make sure you talk respectful — have patched, at least, your jeans.
Use forks for meat, and spoons for soup. Are not, in fact, a slob.
This I've done, with scant results, for though you scrub up pretty
You're rather apt to wreck the show with a dirty little ditty

Or a burst of raucous laughter, generally during Grace:
Mess-hall wit, African tales, wars which seem never to end;
You terrify my daughters, and my wife averts her face

As you pound the table, guzzle our grog, and force us to defend
Our shattered peace with angry looks, and glances at the door.
At 3 a.m. you at last cast off from our bottle-littered shore,

And we are left to ponder if we're better off or worse.
A pretty tough decision, but one we'll have to make.
Would we druther have our mother all alone with whine and curse
Or pile the burden on this other poor infatuated rake?
She, of course, is happy, whatever path we choose,
Her mind's made up, she's flung the dice, she's in there, win or lose.

You're Helen's problem now, of course, I cannot intervene
With the choice she's gone and made — nor would I dare to.
Of course, I've seen sides of her which you have never seen .....
Well, on reflection, maybe not. I wouldn't care to
Speculate on what comes next, sing Hymen's hymn
Too early, or too late, or take John's pleasure from him.

I gather that you love her. Have done, you say, for years.
She says the same, and none here will disbelieve her;
As Heloise of old loved Abelard through memory and tears
Whilst Time stood still in envy. She's yours if you'll have her,
And can tolerate her dreadful family and friends
Like this mob here. We shall try to make amends

To a man we have come to know, then like, then love,
A man to be relied upon, who's always there
When divots fly and swords flash out and pinch gives way to shove,
And the Grim Receiver stalks the door of all our hope and care.
The lone bird cries at night for its helpmeet and its mate;
The piping answer quickens, and the shrivelled world grows great.

You've sat your steed, stout fellow, that I'll give,
And banged your armour angrily when the pace grew warm.
Earned your trinket, earned indeed the right to live
In our poor castle, ivy-ruined, in honey's idle swarm.
So strike those anvils! Let the bells ring! Time rears and twists.
Enter the mad knight, John Quixote, into our lists!

Das Lied von der Erde

for Carl Vine, and for the friend he lost. Ewig, maestro, ewig.

By the Ebro delta, high in the hills,
sits a monastery ruin, languid with weed,
old peasants grub where the cloister lay
and the chapel is littered with thistle and seed;
I imagine the abbot, his monks, and their girls
confessing their pleasure in the grottoes above,
dissolved like their rituals, and melted away
from their temple of labour, and laughter, and love.

And down in Seville, a Pietà stands,
a cunning device cut starkly in wood.
A mother bewails the bewildering loss
of the son she succoured, of all that is good;
and all around the apostles stare
in grief and shock, which has splayed their hands
so they, too, seem to be hung on a cross
of helpless rage, and remorseless despair.

An author, whose plays are like gold beaten thin
is eaten alive by the cancer he bears;
His eyes, pale pitiful pleas, cajole
relief from the cycle which erupts again.
His plays are as subtle as they are cruel,
full of the squalor and sweetness of sin;
Pain has destroyed him — yet from it he tears
the stuff of his art, and his knowledge of men.

A composer I know built an altar of sound
around which he twisted a song without end;
a prayer which is swept to the crest of the heavens,
an elegy mourning his lover and friend.
If music could weep, or seem to at least,
then this is the piece where such fusion is found;
It trembles with beauty, and the sadness which leavens
the pith of our lives with its festering yeast.

Instead of cavorting, like children, in pleasure,
we seem dragged as if hypnotised back to our pain,
and these foils of grief which like icons we treasure
become links in a delicate, piniioning chain.
The wheel of fire we are bound to together
rolls ponderously on as if oiled by our tears;
All our creations, and patient endeavour
turned useless by time, and the withering years.

Yet again creeps that note of ineffable beauty,
like a bird startling up in a flurry of fright,
like the cool, ruined church where the shadows lie long,
like the calm on the face of that dead wooden Christ.
We are driven, it seems, by a strange sense of duty
to harness our losses, yoke up our pain,
and work from them wonders of sculpture and song,
and symphonies rich with their mournful refrain.

An Invitation to Dinner

*Addressed to Mr Les Murray, a Poet of some note, and country squire of
no little weight, who early abandoned the rough and tumble of Concrete
Verse for the more supple variety, and who has been obliged by the arts
hierarchy in Australia to hack his own way up the mountain, working on
the estimable notion that one does not succour or sustain outright talent
in case such largesse* **might somehow kill it off;** *and who, in 1979,
troubled himself to read some of the Author's early verses and, in a brief
note back, even affected to have enjoyed them in places.*

Les Murray liked me poems:
now what d'ye say to *that*!
He read them in an afternoon
and wrote a letter back.

Said "Thank you mister Weller,
for your crudely witty verse,
I've seen a lot that's better,
but also, some that is worse."

And that's from the man whose writing
surges above them all,
thundering winds, with biting
lips, which howl and squall,

yet sudden changing, zephyr-like,
like breezes wafting from heaven,
on which butterflies glide in delight
and flowers are softly driven.

My weak works, visiting him,
arrived with scattered portion;
a mis-spent youth come creeping in;
scruffy Ishmaelite of a cousin.

But Les, whose work has been jeered
by the snivelling little tarts,
and the brats from the FitzRot years,
and doddering Arts Council farts,

who's not Modern, or New Wave, or *Avant*,
whose talent draws forests of sticks
to beat out the life of his poems
and skewer their skins to the bricks,

has decided to enjoy my scribblings;
a weak sally forth for you, son!
I cut no ice with the quislings
who command our Art, and our fun,

nor have cloaked chill limbs in the furry
defence of the burrowing mole,
which our Arts-priests, milky eyes blurry
take as surplice, and cassock, and stole.

I've no fellowships I can deliver,
you could hardly be arse-licking worse.
Would it not be more useful, and clever,
to admire Tom Shapcott's weak verse?

Or Adamson, Dorothy Hewett,
or any dumb, crumb-grubbing ant,
afloat on the mountain-lake sewer
of the endlessly-forming grant?

This is wasted alliance you are seeking,
with an Arab-pack, quick to disperse
when the lumbering legions come shrieking
against you and your vineyards of verse.

But the Bedouin does have his uses,
though not very handy at war,
he's his tent, and felafel, and carpets
spread thick on his soft, sandy floor;

And Les Murray has praised his orisons,
his horses, the wadis he roams;
whilst no acre is his, the horizons
are the borders of all that he owns.

Thus, let the old infidel visit
this patch of dry earth, if he durst;
Sup strange dissertations of spirit,
Put flesh on the bones of his verse.

In short, you're invited to dinner,
though 'twill do you small good, it is true.
The pleasure's all mine, you old sinner,
for what we shall dine on, is you,

and what we shall drink is the laughter
from your crucibles cunning and long;
and finish the feast with liqueur
distilled from the wine of your song.

So thank you, sir, for your letter,
if you come, I shall be *thy* guest,
For who would seek further, or better,
than to drink up the night with the best?

A debt to Ben Jonson acknowledged

for Hal Colebatch, singer of songs

*Here I imagine Will Shakespeare indebted — perhaps after a drinking
session at The Mermaid or some other tavern — by way of tab to his
friend and fellow-playwright, Ben Jonson, who, the day following,
naturally wants back his advance. Scholars of the period will, of course,
be horrified, since Shakespeare was a stout, property-owning bourgeois,
whilst Jonson — bricklayer, actor, murderer, philanderer, scholar,
playwright, and jailbird — was a scrofulous poet similar to our modern,
funded variety (or to what they would like to be), ever without means, and
altogether rotten in his habits. It is possible, however, that Shakespeare,
the consummate businessman, might have cheated Jonson of a significant
sum in their drinking sessions, and that Jonson, unequipped with the
devil's knowledge of business dealings, might have taken mighty offence
at this. Old Silvertongue here attempts to redress the balance (without, it
will be noticed, actually fronting with the readies), suggesting that there
may be life after debt.*

Ah, Ben Jonson, thou shambling ruin, we are no longer friends,
and that doth rile me — nay, enrage me! — something sore.
Such times we had, such laughter spilt on a wine-dribbled floor,
such nonchalant spells of riot, a round without purpose, or end!

Ben, thou lunatic. We have fallen apart on a purse
of tatty gold, which I owe thee, or thou dost me — memory palls.
I try to reckon our bargain, lay up your torrent of sparkling verse
against my cynical wit, and twisted cheer, bleak waterfalls.

I love your plays, old hooligan. I love the way that you sneer
at fool and puritan — at all who would turn to rot
the very stuff of our pleasure, all who would twist, and make queer
our childish glee, our happiness, and our tinkered garden plot.

And I love your ways, and goodly riot, and make-a-setting-to,
and tavern-wisdom, awful slop, and artful, scheming thought.
I miss our drinking sessions, and the shouting derring-do
of our plans to twit this cringing world, and set its crimes to naught.

To fall apart upon money! Why, that's banker's paltry tort,
where owed's malicious, owest crept into nook to darken debt.
Ben, we are artists, surely, our debenture is the world's. We ought
make poetry to settle bills, and songs to hearken yet,

If we were sensible, which we're not, nor will be, thank'ee God!
Galumphing loon, huge with thyself, and thy perpetual frown;
Hast calculated properly thy debts, hast with poke and prod
unpitchforked straw from dung, culled need from all thou'st sown?

Thou gangler, how we drank and sang! How we dangled
life's idiocy on our hip, how we set the maidens ducking
with our riotous song, and bardic zip: how we frightfully mangled
decency, and all that's settled — o, when we went a-fucking

down Eastcheap, did not the very chastened chooks set up a-babble
at our noisy eggings, did not our wives start aggressively up
in angry rumble, did not we, in fact, make of ourselves a scrabble
of muddling men, roosterish, hen-hungry, and keen to sup?

Now seek'st thy penny. 'Tis thine, loon, once I have it in my hand.
I know 'tis this what keeps us fast from the blasted, withered heath.
But for now, my purse is empty — look, it grins at us like a fiend
from hell, slack, hissing thing, glum mouth shorn of its teeth,

and altogether useless in what it can do. Thou wretched bag!
Will Shakespeare is be-shot of thee! Thou hast lost me a friend
'gainst which all your winnings are like love of a withered hag,
and all your former purchasings but a shameful debt without end,

having cost me my Ben, my gentle Ben, my fellow in idle song.
Couldst easy have discharged him, would have done thee little harm.
Wert mean, or cautious, purse, in disaccomodating him?
Was't business, or displeasure, which impelled thy leathery arm?

Ah, fool! Thou hast confused me with my pocket. We do not speak,
our wives will not allow it. We sneer at one another's verse
because we must — after all, we owe it. Can we not sneak
a detour from this stock-exchange, can we not disperse

all we have hazarded and lost in a glorious cacophony of song?
We have joined in such rich chorusings in times gone sadly past,
and chortled up night's velvet black with poems loud and long,
struck heaven's anvil, made shrill clang, and staggered home at last

after wine has thrilled us, verse trilled us, the grog turned us again
away from pain, and our share of loss, the baggage left for the foe,
away from the grubby twilight world of the grey, half-living men,
and the mortgages which cloister them, and trundle 'em to and fro.

Thou rhymester friend, how I owe thee! Money's little matter, lout,
'tis all thy verse what earns thee! I'll be debtor 'til I'm seventy,
and body shrink to slug-a-bed, and weak old whisker sprout,
and my own thin work oil boldly up the foison of your plenty,

gentle Ben, creditable Ben, thou vast, prodigious talent,
receptacle of beauty's dole, thou harvester of dreams,
forgive thy debts, until they're paid, and take what's said as meant.
When old Will Shakespeare gives his word, trust his little means.

Dost think I'd cheat thee, Harlequin? Dost think I'd tear a piece
from Colombine's thin costume, so to keep me wrapped and warm?
Shame upon you, Ben! We were friends now, tipplers for the nonce
round various Brass Monkeys. Ay, man, recoup from that swarm!

Pompilius Aloft

Well, after all that! I quite enjoy being dead,
when you tot it up. There's no one to blame
you for not getting up, or for frigging about,
or for anything, really. Actually, it's the same

as being little, no one seems to care. Probably because
there's no one here. It's all so grey, and flat.
Nor do I know where I am, nor ever really was.
But no one can touch me here. I like that.

Can't take it with you

A poem for teetotallers, bless their little hearts. The last lines are rather
lugubrious nine-beat affairs, and don't fit here, so I've broken 'em up.

"Can't take it with you!" quoth the rubicund tyke
at Sixty Darling Street, our Balmain bottle shop.
Wheedling his customers up and down: "It's cheaper by the case!
Now that Alsatian *Gewurtz* — there's a lovely drop!
oily like, and olive-looking green,
    with a ton of kick. Not bad for a white."

"What's another ten bucks — come on, can't take it with you!"
Not the money, that is. That's only time's thin streams,
measured up in coloured strips — a fool's exchange.
"Sorry, Billy, I need some on account — you're at your limit, see?"
So Billy takes none with him,
    even temporarily. He has not the means.

No, you can't take it with you. True enough, and fair enough,
just out the door, and quickly home, and guzzle down,
and back for more, but not for permanence, or for joy which lasts.
It is but froth and bubble, sustenance, survival's stuff,
a swirl of merriment, perhaps,
    a bluster-up, a gibbering, drunken dream

that's shared by all. Here writers come, who've failed,
and businessmen, bright eyes a-glint with hope's thin seam;
and lonely women, furtively, to eek another sagging cask
from dwindled pension, clutching it with fingers
curdled up with misery,
    each one a question begging to be asked.

All to tap their portion, such as it is. The cases of wine
lie winking in the flickering light, like troops arrayed for the kill.
There is so much pleasure here, so many genies trapped and corked,
each bottle a future tale to tell, of lust-enlivening,
solitary moan, or a rowdy mob
    a-guzzling on like pigs at their sucking swill,

or someone fresh abandoned, clutching the thick skin of glass
as if 'twere sweetheart, cold, but yet unexorcised, half-full of fun.
Or two old doddering, wrinkled things, struggling to pop the cork,
set memory's flute on their flimsy board, about their shrunken feast,
and let viscous fluid play kerosene
                on dwindling flame, to re-ignite their sun.

And all who have need of fancy to tickle their brains, eagerly come,
and offer up their coins as if they were prayers.
Life is short, after all, and the goddess does not offer
much of substance to our mumblings. Let's then fill a bumper up
with rich Falernian wine, such as Senators quaff;
                let's squander it, like Caesar does!

But to take it with you? No. Only as far as home, or home's excuse,
there to sip, or sup, or froth away another night's black, formless air;
no further than your very belly's bank-vault, burping and obtuse.
O, keep children far from hence, lest the things they might become
be pickled up, or drowned
                before they shudder to life in this cauldron of despair.

Plugger

Tony "Plugger" Lockett switched from St Kilda's footy team to the Sydney
Swans in 1995, precipitating one of the most extraordinary sporting
phenomena Australia has witnessed — Sydney actually joining the rest of the
country in the celebration of our national game.

Big and lumpy, mean enough, but an artist of delight,
he plays as the Greeks did, angry, and extreme.
Bashed a few in his time, not afraid of a sprawling fight,
nor wimp in a brawl round the goalposts. The backbone of his team

and the darling of the crowd, which has tired of sensitive men
and their sly embrace. Women go mad about the bugger
as his ludicrous bulk soars in the air like a demon
of svelte, aggressive strength. Yay, Plugger!

Their New Home

She sits in her mountain haunt, and laughs at the moon,
like Meg Merrilees, old gypsy. She loves the hills
and the mountain fog, and the thickly threshing trees.
It is to her an escape out of time, and a rediscovery of him
who, pale and thin in the city, is almost boisterous here.
Like surfing home on a strong wind, aloft on the breeze.

She had grown up in Albany, a tiny town on the coast,
with creeks and magic fountains bursting forth,
and preserved high hopes because of this. Her ideal spot
would be fructive, damp, and rich with furtive rot.
It would be garden, albeit tousled, a windy one
with sprig of lilac springing out of angry earth.

Outside, in a fevered storm, the trees are tossed and swayed
like dancers tangled in leaves, alive with the wind.
She joins their crazy lolloping, and claps her hands
at such wild, witless storm, and in scorn of food
she glares full hard against the bucketing moon.
She is a witch tonight, she has mischief made

under tenty hat, with her wands of hazel twisted.
She is utterly in her element. He, I am afraid,
is unimpressed by winter's blast and drear swoon,
and stokes the fire moodily, to warden chill.
She shivers at the heat he makes, and gazes still
at the pale, silken glitter of the fluctuating moon.

To him, a house like the others, warm and comfortable,
with a chair to sit, and a desk to write his stuff.
Sure, the air is good. In the mountains, it is enough
to breathe the crisp night mist, re-pink your lung.
To wander through the bushland, to vibrate fresh and stable
in one's blood-rush — ai, to feel capable, and young!

But she senses more than this, and stares at the moon
through the twisted trees, through a tangle of desire.
On these mountain slopes, it seems but a breath away
from her grasp, her own invigorating fire.
She swells in its milky light — clutches, and holds it fast.
This time she will hold it to her. She has come home, at last.

Old Photographs

Old photographs, time to toss you
with all the other junk. Time to move.
Little room for nostalgia in our new house,
so out you go! What's this old thing?
Good god! Did I ever dress in such gaudy rags
and spruik such waterfall of tangled hair?
Look at that dumb, self-satisfied grin!
Young men should not read books,
nor toy with art, nor indeed, do anything
at all on camera, it becomes them not.
Here's old homes I have lived in, faded out
of plastic thought, and friends I have forgot.
Here's muddle o' happiness, for no one thought
to photograph the blackness when it fell,
nor capture with these thin scraps of celluloid
the brief glimpses into the turbulence of hell.
No, they are happy, beaming shots
of happy, if hapless, youths and moody girls
poignant with worry whether to breed or not.

There, all packed in a crumbling box
which can go with the rest to the public tip.
I cannot bear to keep, and index you
in such fixed sort, to be hauled out
in years to come, to say "Look, here's you,
and you, and you!". What I'll do, instead,
is affix, this time more faithfully,
these oblong memories in my scrapbook head.

I know thee not

FALSTAFF: My king! My Jove! I speak to thee, my heart!

KING: I know thee not, old man. Fall to thy prayers,
How ill white hairs become a fool and jester!
I have long dreamt of such a kind of man,
So surfeit-swelled, so old, and so profane,
But being awaked, I do despise my dream.

Shakespeare, Henry IV, Part II

*Henry V, formerly young Prince Hal, to his old friend and drinking
companion, Sir John Falstaff, a coward, braggart and wastrel. Here
Falstaff explains this apparently callous rejection to his friends Shallow,
Pistol, Bardolph and Nym, demonstrating an exemplary understanding of
the vicissitudes of power, and perhaps something of its loneliness.*

Nay, nay, 'tis but colic, Master Shallow,
or newly kingly come, he *plays* at seems!
In fact, he *must* be thus. He talks of his dreams
in which I figure boldly — marked ye that?

My pretty, playful Hal! Look at him, Nym:
how graceful is his lively countenance!
In regalistic posture, every scrap a king:
such power in his bearing, such edict in his glance!

'Tis but politics. He remembers well
our rowdy farts and wine-slopped rollickings.
And Mistress Quickly's sack — o, he'd burn in hell,
forgetting that, or our lusty bollickings.

Nay, foolish Pistol, he is not dead,
our sapling prince, by bulging out to King!
His bark has swelled, a crown sprung on his head,
he rears and glares preposterously, but it is still him.

He speaks so to reform us — the mark of a king
once idle fancy's gone. I tell you, he loves us
more than ever, more than in youth's mad fling
round our taverns, with our leery japes and rumpus.

Sure, he has put it harsh, and painfully.
I know thee not, old man! Has an awful ring
hast not? To some would seem like cruelty.
But not to Falstaff. 'Tis fair part of everything

to shuffle out your court cards. No, I'm glad for him
to have shot so high, so quick, so sudden, too.
His words were hard, but his eyes sang secret hymn
of forget-me-not, methought. Seemed not to you?

Ah, 'tis evil to be old! All honour fled
to shambling limb and gibbering lip and watery eye.
Echoes of laughter, friends grown king, or dead,
one's every move an effort not to die.

Of course he dis-remembers! He is whore no more
to Eastcheap's raucous muckabout, and seedy sin.
He'll maybe hold it in him, though, as store
of sweet provision 'gainst a chilly wind,

as courtier friends turn enemy in frightful twist
and sons erupt in homicidal plot.
Thou'll greed for memory then, and ribald bliss,
fond, puppety king, what knows me not!

And I'll be there, God willing, to revive those days
a-babbling 'a green fields, and a-gorging sack.
Your throne a stool again, where you loll and laze
in shabby splendour, fussed by your faithful Jack,

and all the world shall be banished thence, 'cept us,
Pistol, Poins and Shallow, yes, and Bardolph, too.
Your mirthy sycophants, who will deck and truss
your grace in hessian-robes to pay our due.

Small kingdom, that, and weakly served, yet strong
in love and laughter's troops, whom you've forgot.
And none to sudden throw thee, after ruling loud and long
with those words to pierce thy very heart: *Old man, I know thee not.*

Ah, city in the sand dunes, thou art sick with mottled spite,
for your people, living fabric, hate the very smell of you.
Although they cling like barnacles, they would leave you in a trice
if the world but beckoned to them, which it will never do.
There is no-one nigh nor loves you such as to give advice
or send you troops in a crisis. No succour nor respite
when slobbertooth comes to sack you, and fold you in endless night.

Mel is feeding the maggies

Mel is feeding the maggies, and they gulp at her proffered meat.
Their wings clip-clap in confusion, as they scrabble with angry feet.
The cat stares wide-eyed in horror, as his enemies circle around,
fed by his fondling hand, soothed into neutral ground.

Mel is feeding the maggies, and from every branch they flit
'til the ground is black with jostling beaks, and thick with their shit.
The cat slopes off in a frightful huff, nose in the squawk-filled air.
There's trouble for possum and mice tonight. Ye innocent, beware!

Its tail flicks up as it leaves the room, and its bum doth hiss
a contemptuous, grumpy fart, at its Mistress behaving like this.
'Tis the mindless rage, and seethe of disgust, of a jilted cat.
But Mel is feeding the maggies, and nothing must clash with that.

The other cats have given up — they sulk in their gloomy dens,
or mooch about in the kitchen, and dream of their bleak revenge.
For Mel must soon travel to Sydney, and let them loose for the day,
and maggies will learn what it means to be toy to the pussycat play.

And Mel will return to scattered wisps of birdies littered and torn,
rent by her dear little moggies into carcasses forlorn.
Mel will stop feeding the maggies, when she sees she is the cause
of luring them close with innocent joy, into hell's pink jaws.

A Trip in the Country

heading to Bridgetown in the old Kombi, 1974. For Sean & Sheila.

Therefore I say unto you, Take no thought for your life, what ye shall eat, or what ye shall drink; nor yet for your body, what ye shall put on. Is not the life more than meat, and the body than raiment? Behold the fowls of the air; for they sow not, neither do they reap, nor gather into barns; yet your Heavenly father feedeth them. Are ye not much better than they?

Therefore, take no thought saying, What shall we eat? or What shall we drink? or Wherewithal shall we be clothed? Your heavenly Father knoweth that ye have need of all these things.

Take therefore no thought for the morrow: for the morrow shall take thought for the things of itself. Sufficient unto the day is the evil thereof.

Matthew 6, 24-34 (condensed a little)

Bouncing about in our Volkswagon Kombi,
purple flowers plastered on the side.
Beards and brandy and girls with thighs like honeypots,
the air thick with talk and smoke.

Colour, colour everywhere! Rich, thick yellows
dabbed in paint, or the erupting sheen
of beaten gold in a girl's cascade of hair.
Turquoise shirts, and trousers of bright tangerine.

A luscious sense of living, of being alive
and young and careless, atop of a world
spinning crazily to destruction, with George Grosz
its portraiturist, Bob Dylan its poet.

Hushed talk of parents, poor floundering things
with hungry teeth bared against loneliness,
desperate claws outstretched to grimly cling
to their very spawn, in their bitterness.

Night settling in a purple haze. The moon a knife
of gold in a velvet cushion of stars.
Musk snuffled in nostrils. A moist patch of life
in a girl's sweet complexity of crotch.

No more brandy. A half bottle of Scotch,
a flagon of sour red wine, and a bagful of dope.
Laughter in the back, as the van buckets on
through the towering trees like a space probe.

Ah, such energy, such sweet delight!
The van a living sculpture, a riot of art
and consciousness, a pod of blazing light
in the black and loveless void it careers across,

heading nowhere, headless and without cause
or purpose, just a bunch of kids
full of life's rich juice, with laughing jaws,
bonging and banging their way to Bridgetown.

Song of an Utter Pervert

for T.S. Eliot

I've had me share of relationships, and other poofy stuff,
I've raised me fucking consciousness, high as high.
I'd attend a bloody pregnancy class, if pinch came to snuff.
But to fuck a pretty woman: for that I'd die.

I shouldn't really grizzle, or babble on like this.
I haven't had much luck with girls, I dunno why.
I s'pose I'm weak at wooing when I've hit the bloody piss.
But to hump a pretty woman: for that I'd die.

I'd like to be a warrior, a real bloody lout.
Stagger home all sick with gore, and popping eye.
With a sack of booty I could casually shake out.
But to soak a pretty woman: for that I'd die.

I hate me job at the Bank. It makes me sick
To sneak about in creaseless shirt and Paisley tie.
The girls bend over the money desks, and their bottoms flick
like lackey bands: o, to stick me dick up some of that, and die!

Shit. They giggle at me acne, and me long, thin neck.
I'm a figure of fun to them, and I know damned why.
I'd love to drag their panties off, and spread 'em across the deck!
Just a finger up their warm, moist crotch: for that I'd die!

I'd be as good a husband as the bitches could expect.
I'd meet the mortgage, pay the bills, and generally try
To keep domestic order. And I'd be circumspect.
But to fuck my little woman: oh, I'd sink back and die.

Of course, I'd want her tame and delicious. And just for me.
I'd want her mesmerised, under my gimlet eye.
I would want to gloat at her being mine, my property.
And I would want to fuck her endlessly. For that, I'd die.

And not just fuck her, no: I'd like to muck her about
However I wished, jam candle-stubs up her arse, and cry
With happy savagery as I lit 'em, and made her shout
And scream with the shrieking pain: ah, for that I'd die.

Yes. Then stuff it up her blistered, blackened hole,
and tear her ear half off as I did, and twist her tits awry.
Revel in her whimpering, and triumph in my role
as her Devil Master, Lord of Pain, where I'd bulge and die!

Small chance, with these tight-arsed cunts at the Bank.
Their skirts slide up to their rumps along stockinged thigh.
They are tempting, taunting me, who would spunkily spank
their wriggling little buttocks: ah, for that I'd die!

But I have no luck with women, as I've agreed and said.
For some reason they seem to shudder, and pass me by.
These useless slits at the Bank, who sneer, and cut me dead.
God, I'd love to fuck one, just one, before I die.

For John Berryman

1. His Toy

He was grand in his fashion, like grizzled Hemingway,
although dribbling into his porridge, gurgling his tea.
Not even a poet's arsehole, he'd splutter, morning-mad.
She clicked about him like a wind-up doll, making him sad
with her clatter and chatter, making him see
o so clearly what a fool he'd become to his dingle-dongle whim.
But glad, glad. Her wiggle of hip just blew him away.

So why did he leave her, or she him?

2. His Dream

His eyes were like sultanas, pale green in the night,
shrunk, pipless things. Through them he drank her in
as she floated all about him with her creamy hair
taunting the muttering moon. He sank with a sigh into sin,
stretched bony, sensitive fingers into this lust of light.
Felt nothing there, found the raging lay within
his supine form, and came shuddering up for air.

O why did he leave her, or she him?

3. His Rest

The water spreads out like a mirror — I can see there
a thousand lives like mine stare grimly back at me.
Jeer not, you watery watchers, I'll jump amidst ye,
hide, hide, like my father did, in the billowy tide
with the weed and the shells and the coral combing my hair.
Deep into thee I'll thrust myself, and sweetly swim
far from this woman of world. Or so he lied.

But why did he leave her, or she him?

Aussie Drinking Song (Cairo 1942)

Dulce et decorum est pro patria mori [*Horace*]

> *Booze, boys, let's go hit the booze.*
> *We've coins in our pocket, and a limp, shrivelled prick.*
> *We've nothing to win, boys, and nothing to lose.*
> *Let's blizzard our innards, and drink ourselves sick!*

I've had it with Gippos, they give me the shits.
They're greasy and sour, and their women are dogs.
They've gave me the clap, and they've given me nits
whilst sucking me pay, the dark, slimy wogs.

And I've had it with Cairo, foul city of sin,
they told me it stank, and they told me no lies.
But they never did tell me how rotten and thin
were its whores and its pimps, with their mean little eyes.

> *So let's hit the booze, boys, let's give it a whirl,*
> *Let's stick it up Gip's thin hairless brown arse,*
> *and when finished with him, let's grab us a girl*
> *from the wrong end of town, and stuff her with glass.*

I wish I were back in old Ballarat town,
with Maisy O'Grady a'serving us beer,
old Paddy O'Shea a-glugging 'em down
as if Christmas were every damned day of the year.

Where the gum trees grow tall, in a great, graceful sweep,
and the river banks gleam like a mine of rich clay,
Where the earth still holds gold you can fossick and keep,
and the girls drift like swans through the heat of the day.

> *No, let's hit the booze boys, in old Cairo town,*
> *and hit like a howitzer loosing its shell,*
> *lets burst on these Ay-rabs like fire raining down*
> *and show 'em a glimpse of our down-under hell.*

God give me strength to live with this.
Yet how can he give aught, who snatcheth all
in one quick grab? Is he so blind
he would trample on his garden shoots, or so cruel
that he would toy with me, as boys
cavort with flies? Does he dodder
in his dotage? Sweet Lord, does my Hamnet die
whilst thou dost sleep, or on some hellish whim?

I loved thee, lithesome creature. Cry peace
to thy heap of bones, now thy tiny soul is free.
Peace to whatever phantom thou now art,
or will come to be.

God bear me witness, I hereby snap my pen.
Will Shakespeare has been emptied out
of happiness, and life's rich draught.
He'll potter, he'll smile, and nod to acquaintance:
oh, he'll *seem* to live!

But the heart lies cold in this moving coffin
which lurches and slips o'er the ice.
No. The trickster is beshot of his verse.
He'll not weave again his cheery quips
nor rehearse the cast of his vice.

Coriolanus, a Roman epitaph

We had no use for him, or what we had is spent
and gone from memory's fickle purse. He is none
of our persuasion since he fled us, and to the Volsci lent
his terrible passion for war. He has certainly done

what we feared most, and rained upon our city
our own sick lust for pillaging rape and gore.
I hear that his villains murdered him. 'Tis pity
we were ourselves too weak to honour him more.

Three Poems for Kings

Kings have had, I think, a somewhat rum time of it throughout history, and have in the main been poorly served by their chroniclers. Apart from Alfred, there are few amongst our English ones held in any sort of esteem, and the continent is equally morose about its former rulers. In Africa, however, parts of Asia, and throughout the South Pacific, a different tradition prevails, whereby former kings are usually revered unto many generations of their passing. It is possible we have been too harsh on ours — they had a difficult task to perform, and generally a thankless one. Certainly they were obliged to carry heavy burdens, and could not retire like a politician, although a tiny handful of them managed this extraordinary feat (including Philip of Spain's father, Charles). I wonder how many of them, with the prospect of a decent retirement on a solid government pension, and the safety of their person guaranteed at law by the incoming administration, might have taken up such an option?

1. Charles Stuart, In Prison

for Alec Guinness

Go soft, little bird on my window-sill, as you fluff out your breast,
and peck at my generous bounty, these hard, brittle lumps of bread.
Fly thee on delicate wings to your rooks and eaves in the west.
Sing songs of the prince in his prison, sing of the king who is dead.

Let your twittering sound like a bugle call, but not to arms,
since we're gorged with war. Instead, sound thy tinsel flute
as requiem to folly, and avarice, and the power which charms
us from our cradles into crabbed old men, crippled with loot.

Parliament, by God! 'Tis full of hangdog men
who'd sell their souls for money. Ay, 'tis already done.
I am the Law, express through them. They have crushed and broken
both it and me, as a boy squashes flies with his thumb.

Do not eye me beadily, thou courtier bird. You've got
all I can simple fee from out my shrunken hoard.
No, wait. Here's cheese for thee, a dry old chip. I forgot
I held such fief not yet allotted, or such regal board.

You have seen better kings, you think. Ay, that I'll grant,
small aeronaut, for thou art more richly bred than us.
Perched on his crag is your eagle, aloft is your cormorant,
and high above heaving palace of sea floats the albatross,

and every fragile, feathered speck is king to itself
or queen to her loving lord, who conquered, lords over him.
None rule thee, guileless thing, nor hast thee for thyself
one solitary, pecking servant, nor priest, nor seraphim.

My dear, loyal cavaliers, who fought when the cause was lost!
The worst among them still living, the best amongst whom are dead.
I would they had not risen again, for it has cost
this Solomon his glory, and this weak-witted king, his head.

Nay, press not in these narrow struts, thou'll like it not
to share this cage and live like a king behind these bars.
Your careless song would be scattered here, your wings would rot
as we became two mindless, chattering budgerigars.

For here they lop off the heads of that which they dread, and hate,
which would serve thee ill. We label this intelligence, and claim
dominion of the world in consequence. You would rate
it simply bestial, since it has no point, nor aim.

Hai! Snap not up at my fingers, princeling bird
or I'll cancel out this harvest-tide of heavenly crusts!
Like me, art thou discontent to possess the entire world
in simple peace, and careless rule with thy beak's deft thrusts?

And like me, art greedy ever yet for ever more,
some principle of perfect rule which comes from God?
Some useless, gilded thing, a gift of bloody war
to the man who grinds my flour, and the hand which turns my sod?

Ah, I am a weak and foppish king! To die
with nothing done, or won; to roll over like a whore
that's whipt for stealing purse; to prevaricate, to lie
to bald-headed lawyer-men, so to live a little more!

To have lost so much, due to foolishness, or worse!
My people loved me: how could I toss aside such a crown?
Am I simply out of fashion? Has this terrible, popular curse
called Parliament outpeopled me, and brought me down?

Methinks it has, Robin Redbreast, little friend to a friendless king.
Ay, pluck at thy crumbs! I have confused policy with pleasure,
and art with both, in my idle, aimless fossicking;
have virtue made of futility, and an icon of leisure.

To fearful folk like Cromwell, these crimes are huge, and resemble
play in the pits of hell, where devils prance like kings.
They are honest, misguided, puny men, who cannot dissemble
their terrible fear of beauty, of all which cavorts and sings,

and magnificence is such stuff to them as to send them mad.
Perhaps they are right. I am sure that sitting here, little featherkins,
glum Oliver, even, would gravely nod at your fussing, and be glad
that God should send his tormented world such delicate things.

My slender neck feels stout and thick beneath my head.
Tomorrow they'll cut us adrift, and bundle us into the earth.
That's the way of men. Bustle off little creature, to thy downy bed.
I am tired of this living. I have earnt what I am worth.

2. Charles of Sweden

Charles XII of Sweden (born 1682, reigned 1697-1718) spent most of his kingly life at war abroad. He was considered one of the greatest warriors of his time, and successively defeated the Danes, the Russians (where he routed Peter the Great's forces at Narva), the Poles and Saxons. In 1707 he invaded Russia again, defeated them at Holorsezyu, and advanced upon Moscow, but turned south before reaching that city. The winter of 1708 was particularly bitter, and the sufferings of the Swedes were unimaginable. Food failed them, and the ravages of winter became so fierce they could not keep themselves warm. When the frost broke, and the Russians attacked, the Swedes were practically annihilated, and Charles with the remnant of his army took refuge in Turkey, where he remained 1709-1714. He had great influence there, causing the Turks to declare war on Russia no less than three times. However, he became troublesome to the Turks, and quit their country in 1714 to finally return to Sweden. In 1717 he attacked the Norwegians, and was shot in the trenches the following year whilst leading an expedition against them.

Across the steppes of Russia I lead on my little band,
and we have our local victories. This segment or that
of this uncompromisingly vast and bewildering land
falls now to Sweden, and then uncompromisingly back.

Back, back to the Russia it ever was, and will ever hugely be.
What on earth are we doing here? Can I really take
this monstrous stretch of bog and slush, and turn its policy
to little Sweden's? Will it, or will I, break?

Peter the Tsar keeps outpointing me, and he seems
to carry this large land with him. They have turned to him.
Perhaps they sense a nationhood, and have laced their dreams
with the strong liqueur of Russianness, in which they swim.

Yet the *Rus* were Swedish rowers, who settled in Kiev,
which is strange for Northmen. I am here on behalf of my kin.
We have ever swept unto foreign shores, and have left
a litter of looted church and huts in our beggaring.

I sit in my drizzling tent, and gaze at this field
of snow and mud, with the odd little clump of tree.
I will un-number these Russians, and will never yield
to the obvious, or the ludicrous, or to destiny.

I am Charles of Sweden, the mightiest warrior left on earth,
and my men are the last of the Vikings, fierce and lean.
They had better kill me first, to establish what I am worth,
for I budge not from this conquest, mad as it seem.

Back home, in my distant fief, my people grind and till,
and bicker the ice, and my awesome land, as they would with skalds.
Their battle resembles mine, and will last until
the sun turn North in its wild course, and melt their fields.

My soldiers are clumped about me here, and they question not
what I order them, or what battles we enter next.
They are gruff at their lack of booty, but have grasped the plot
of their flickering fate, and can read its runic text.

Rowers and brigands no more, they have slowly but surely become
an army with nothing to win or lose but its endless wars.
Their purpose is clean, though forgotten. They are now at one
with the whims of their puppet's head, and the stretch of his claws.

And I, who am leading them here, in this fruitless cause?
Ah poet, you ask me to trill you the tune of your own sweet strings!
A song you must make of my scattered and hopeless wars,
and a saga to thrill down the years of the triumph of kings.

3. In the Escorial

Philip II of Spain reigned from 1546-1598 after his father Charles V abdicated his throne and empire, and retired to prayer. Philip was a gloomy, morose sort of King, and something of a queer cove. He built the vast palace of the Escorial in the mountains outside of Madrid, theoretically to avoid the summer heat, but in fact to try and escape the monster bureaucracy he had created which, in several senses, absorbed him. He married, amongst others, Bloody Mary Tudor of England, but neither had much fun o' the matter.

Blow, wind, across this darkening sky,
and swirl these clouds in angry banks until
they blot you up, that forming, you might die.
You are but air what whistles through my head,
not real at all, nor warm, nor dangerous.
You snort and puff the winter's bitter chill,
bustling on in hectic busyness,
and flit like a cackle of mirth o'er a world which is dead.

To every life there comes this summer's end,
the cold creep in to every nook of warmth;
the bright diapason of day distend
in the lengthening gloom of the evening's shadowy dread;
young blood grow thick with worrying, to clot
adventure in its veins, and whimpering stealth
around a dwindling fire be all we've got.
Huddle close to that flicker of flame, ye living dead.

I was king of the universe, lord of it all
and all therein. Philip the Glum, of Spain.
Armadas I set on the ocean, and in my thrall
lay a tumbletown of worlds yanked by my thread.
But mine was a barren spring, and my flowers shrank
as I tended them, and their sprouts were but tendrils of pain.
Even God looked on, and laughed, as my galleons sank,
and mocked my prayers with legions of watery dead.

No woman loved me queerly, nor sought to please:
No queen for spindly Philip. My subjects hate me
as a withered, useless, bumbling king, whose knees
knock with winter's creak in their royal bed.
They disgust me utterly, this huddle of men
who haunt my decaying hulk in pursuit of their fee.
They think the sun is in me, and will be in them
by reflection's force, to lift them up from the dead.

They are snowflakes merely, melting as they fall
and mixing in with earth's remorseless dew.
There is not man alive in Spain I'd call
compañero, whom I could not buy with an ounce of lead.
This garden is poisonous creatured, and its roots
are sunk in an icy evil, hidden from view.
I toss my crown like a leaf to this wind which hoots
and groans like the demon choir of the living dead.

Sea Fever

upon reading Masefield again

I must get down to the seas again, to the stark coast line,
Where froth cascades upon the rock, and the air is thick with brine;
And all I ask is an hour to walk alone on this seething shore
In the ecstasy that the seagull feels as it swoops and soars once more.

I must get back to the seas again, to that surge that churns within,
As the sudden turn of the current sucks me in and out again;
And all I ask is to be at one with those rhythms of the sea
Which wash about my loneliness, and make flotsam out of me.

I must repair to the seas again, to that dark, forbidding beach
Where the mindless waves come crashing in, chuckling each to each;
And all I ask is the rich, black joy come bubbling out of the foam
As night enfolds this speck on the sand, swept to its swirling home.

An Australian infantryman foresees his death

In Memoriam Herbert Irving, d. Flanders 1917, aged eighteen.

I know that I shall meet my death
awash in this sea of mud and slime,
this trickling stream of soft, sweet breath
turn liquid red, and choke me.
Death will be dreary, not sublime,
though memories fond will cloud my rest:
our mud-brick house on its gravel crest,
the gum, and river oak tree;

Father, marooned in that weird bush
and my Mother dear, strong, bustling thing.
What led them from Surrey, to blindly push
into prickly-poison land?
Was it to hear the magpies sing
in throttled choirs, in their ocean of trees?
Or to sniff clean smoke on the murmuring breeze
as they tilled their acres of sand?

In hell's hot mouth, where the whizz-bangs spit
they are distant, these visions of pleasure and love.
We are up to our knees in Beelzebub's shit
and flies breed thick in the dead.
The shriek of the shells as they shatter above
and the screams of the wounded — this is the song
that Lucifer sings to his children, and strong
is his ghastly summons to bed.

These men I am fighting, and instructed to hate,
are but children like me and my friends over there.
We are beaten for being, and can see, far too late,
how we're tricked of our toys.
If only our guns could be turned on the lair
of the old, and the wicked, who have lured us here
from their murderous dreams, and the creaking fear
they feel for their boys.

'Tis them that I guard, not my shimmering land,
nor the people I love: they would have none of this.
My rifle a stick in my trembling hand,
my bayonet a scrap of string.
I am but a ghost. A few will miss
my being there, but Australia
will heave along regardless, and her banksia
still riot in the spring.

I wish that I could say that I
was led here by some inner urge;
to balance all, and balanced die
in a poet's ecstatic fashion.
You could then leave off your mournful dirge
for wasted youth, and futile crime,
and celebrate the defeat of Time
in my tiny burst of passion.

But nothing so mature as this
could fill the soul of a simple youth
who would lustily live, and drunken kiss
the rich, wet lips of girls.
I am witness now to an awful truth
having seen the black shore of the devil's redoubt,
and the tide of a life scarce begun drain out
in ever-retreating swirls.

There's a Digger nearby in this foul, muddy trench
with a mouth-organ, carolling ditties of home.
The smell of the camp-fire conquers the stench
of this foreign slaughter-sty.
This mug of warm tea is the Chalice of Rome,
encrusted with diamonds of sugar. I suck
at its leafy meniscus, and slurp at my luck.
Tomorrow, at dawn, we die.

Gunpowder, Treason and Plot

for the 5th November Memorial Ceremony which I, at least, maintain. And
specifically for Reg Withers, the gentle Toecutter.

Parliament on the radio — listen to them scream
their tin-shit whistles at each other across their shed.
Like roosters mad in their coop, with some hens joined in
to madden up their cackle, and make shriller din.
They exist as if in some odd, surreal dream
and formless flit through the ether like the living dead.

There is not a cock amongst 'em what will raise its head
in aught but flip-flop anger, for to dribble its wit.
Just their pay and their pension moves them — outside of this
there is naught but a crowding together in a puddle 'o piss.
This is the curdled cream from the teat of the cow which is dead,
wrung from a pail all kicked of its hooves, and sloshed with its shit.

"But you put us here!" they cry, as they wriggle their bums
in democratic rectitude, like a know-all wife.
Not I, you pack of curs. I have never voted yet
and never will while the likes of you are what I'd get.
I'd a rascal King, rather, or a pack of Jewish mums
pull the purse-strings of the exchequer, and of my life.

Here's a Labor leader, cadaverous and thin,
and full of holy prattle of the Working Man.
Woollahra now, his mansion, and his wife Society's queen.
Here's a tiny little Tory: and how *he* doth preen
in this stockbrokers' heaven he has landed in.
To feed 'emselves sick on our Treasury — could that be the plan?

I think on old Guy Fawkes tonight, and I toast him in beer,
since that's all that taxes and duties have left in my drum.
I wonder he played such a solo — was a tyro in fact
in the not unimportant political venture he backed.
I wish he'd had joy of his venture, and I wish the mad cunt was here
to blow this whole fucking chookhouse to kingdom come.

In Memoriam

a fantasy, for Peter, who died of AIDS in Perth some years ago. R.I.P,
thou gentle and thoroughly loveable man.

Ah, thou fond and callow youth,
what warmed me well, and turned my head.
Thou lovely, slender thing. In truth
thou livest yet, though thou art dead.

I must make joy of this, they say.
We loved outrageously, and so
should triumph at the end o' the day.
We were famous dicks, as such things go

and showed the world a trick or two
it might have missed in its muddled play.
We were geese together, partnering through
our tacky squabbles. And we were gay.

Ha! That soft and hopeful word!
You used it often, downy chick.
I laughed at it, and called absurd
your hot and meaty politick.

Now, as we lower you into your grave
where thin you'll lie, and blister, and rot,
we bury passion with you, and shave
our memory clean in this churchyard plot.

How you would have hated this!
Your halfwit mother, terrified to find
herself and your lover partners, to kiss
me like a leper, horrified, but kind.

Your father, stern and ominous,
puzzled that his son could be
so different from him. His curse
hovers curious, and descends on me.

Your sisters, glad it is not them
whose time is up, who can still exult
in this petty victory, but whose phlegm
flies thick at me from their female cult.

Ah, Peter mine, how I loved thee!
Thou wert a salve to this hideousness.
Thou wert like breath, like food to me
who soaked you up in greediness.

They glare at me through this tendering
of homage, as if I were to blame,
and our very, blissful buggering
were author to this hymn of pain.

They are like insects crawled inside
your sad, cheap coffin. I sit
awkwardly alone, off to the side
of your death party, and outside of it.

Never more to hold thee, or to touch
thy soft, white bits! Or to feel thee
groping for me, or to hear such
sweet things as you'd whisper tenderly!

Just not to have you by me, or to grasp
your thickening cock, or stroke thy face.
Not bicker over breakfast, or clasp
you afterwards in glad embrace!

I shall miss thee, idle leprechaun,
your futile cackle, and your ill-baked bread.
I shall be solo now, and forlorn
my nights and mornings, in my single bed.

Well down the queue, I drop a flower
upon you, and hear its tiny thud.
They think our love has killed you, and sour
is the glare of the priest at this mock of his God.

But I shall reverence thee, my love,
in crystal water tinted with wine;
and carol thee sweet, o my turtle-dove,
in this silent requiem of mine.

They snicker at me, as I shuffle out
this mausoleum of your little death.
The ageing poofter, who, without doubt
breathed upon you his poisonous breath.

They are right, in a way. Our love proved
too clean and swift for this sick world.
And palsy took it, once it was moved
to its bitter fate, and to chaos hurled.

So let them judge. We did no harm
to each or other, nor to anything.
We did but love, and each the other charm
with laughter's talisman, and magic ring.

Farewell, thou little mannequin,
and friend of mine, and of my bed.
The world has shrunk, and grown a thin
and rasping place, now thou art dead.

Positively Pompilius' Last Word

It's a terribly dreary thing, wafting through seamless space
in an ectoplasmic orgy, when I'd rather be rooting girls.
I am not cut for this caper, nor can fill this awesome place
with my faded sense of adventure, or my vague, preposterous swirls.

I am told they might send me back! Ah, to revisit that shore
by my inky sea, with my crinkled vines, and my vases shiny!
Please God (whom I've yet to meet) grant body and wit once more
to Pompilius, thy servant, whose sins were obscure, and tiny.

Double Sonnet for my Darling

for Melody, on her 45th birthday, February 15th, 1996, and in apology for the fact that after fifteen years together I have never provided the opportunity for her to mortgage up her future, excepting only once, when the bank foreclosed angrily, 'though justly, after fourteen consecutive non-payments of their monthly expectation; and, I suppose, altogether wishing things had been otherwise, and more respectable.

Half way there, old girl, if you're aiming at hitting ninety.
And why should you not? My great-aunt Ethel managed this,
despite her bustling nieces guarding her estate,
and her as well, reluctantly, who tarried to die.
How they must have hated her! Old, wrinkled tart
who lived and lived, 'til they grew old and grey as her
they'd come to bury decently, when they were young.
You ferret through your lost and littered things, and mutter
at this missing bit, and that, and marvel at what's kept.
You really have no property, to stickle you
in this cobweb world, or mesh you in its architrave.
Your things are broken, flimsy, and few, like the rescued wealth
of an isolated abbey, after Northmen have sucked it dry.
Your altars are decked with silver scraps, and slivers of cats-eye.

To have lived this long, and garnered up so little bounty!
'Tis not the Australian way. They will sneer and jeer at this,
togethered up, in their mortgaged way, in the strings of their fate,
who dangle their puppet's luck, in the hope it will learn to fly.
You, who have gathered nothing, save the tumble of your art,
and the jumble of your books, whose spines you bend and blister;
some Afghan carpets, thick and greasy, cunningly spun,
and yards of bric-a-brac, to make a collector stutter.
The treasure we have hidden from the savages who leapt
from our sleepy coasts to ravage us, les parvenus.
So stripped of our cloth, and ornament, we shall creep to the grave
as naked as we started hence, in cautious stealth.
We shall never own our letterbox, nor stand and eye
our wide demesne with its rolling hills, with servants hovering by.

Abide with me

for Inez Irving

Abide with me, as falls the eventide.
Night's dark silk enfolds me — Lord with me abide.
Earth's warmth has petered out: now I trust in thee,
Thou hearth of the helpless, o abide with me.

Like a candle spluttering out comes close of day,
and joy itself grows truculent, and fades away.
The room grows cold and dark with death's bleak misery.
O thou whose flame is never spent, abide with me.

I am not worthy in thy sight, nor plead a glance
from thy great vision's mystery. Nor would I chance
my soul, as you did yours, upon the Tree.
I die as the Robber died, Lord, apart from thee.

I lie in this darkened room, and feel murmurings
kind and good, with the healing of thy wings.
Is it palsy's grip what shakes my cheek, or your delicacy?
Thou soft and subtle Godliness, reside with me.

Through all a life I can but dim recall aright
there flitted in a sense of thee, like filtered light.
As darkness closes on me now, my eyes grow free
and glowing is the spectrum that glides o'er me.

My fears and woes seem little now, with thy caress
which sweeps away life's twisted loss, and bitterness.
Alone at last, my soul calls out in a hidden ecstasy
to thee my bounden Lord, alongside of me.

Brush over me, thou mighty force, and sweep me clean
of all the dirt and filth my littered life has been.
Death hath no sting in thy embrace, nor grave no victory
as thou gatherest up those petals which have died in thee.

An Injunction upon Lyn, to paint Rod

for Lyn Moran, who has seen and felt all poetry has to offer

Paint him, as he cross and grumpily is.
Paint his brows, which quicken with debate,
and hunch him up into vector, and dilate
as the brush soft washes him o'er with its oily fizz.

Catch the firmness of him, with a lick of white
in his glaring eyes; yes, capture that.
And the worm within, that the world is never quite
what he planned for it, raw Jehosophat.

And get his beard so, that fuzz of fur
what juts upon his chin: 'tis an angry burst
of bristle 'gainst this world of quaint demure.
Paint him crudely discontent. 'Twill be a first

amongst his portraitists, whose paint runs thin.
They pick him for a lackey, sensing need.
They oscillate his virtue, and thus sounding him
they pluck his brains as they would a fulgent weed.

So paint him as he is. As Chay would see
the half-wit lumbering father-thing she'd rather not.
Draw him away from himself, and create him to be
this rock which he is: your thesis, and your plot;

And paint him, Lyn, as the Masters paint, with a sense
of triumph peering out of his angry glare.
Paint him as we love him, in the innocence
of his rage, and his deep commitment, and his wells of care.

From the Scrolls of Shi Hwang-ti

"For a time there was no emperor, but in 249 B.C. the Ts'in dynasty, from which the name of China is derived, had its beginning. Chwang-siang-wang, the nominal founder of this dynasty, died in 246 B.C., and was succeeded by Shi Hwang-ti, the first of the 'universal emperors'. This emperor set himself to do away with the feudal system, and to do this he beheaded some hundreds of the scholars, among whose ranks the system found its chief supporters. To him is attributed the building of the Great Wall, and he is also said to have made many canals etc. For many centuries the Chinese had been engaged in warfare with the Hiang-nu, probably connected with the Huns, and Shi Hwang-ti led a successful expedition against this tribe, driving them into Mongolia." [Everyman's Encyclopaedia, J.M. Dent & Sons, London, 1932]

A grey light falls across China as I consider my sons
and rate their fitness to rule. They have none,
not of knowledge, nor warcraft. They flit
like moths before candlelight, agog at the blaze:
they would be emperors all, and there is not one
amongst them who would swallow the rest
out of greed, or the rectitude of saintliness.
Soft petals dropped from the flower which hangs above the stream
with its nodding head all drowsy in the summer's haze,
they are but perfumed wisps of the incandescent sun.

Bring on the feast, ye scurriers, ay — bring on the feast!
I shall dine three golden days with my mandarins.
Dove's eggs cunningly cooked, and frail, frissonned rice
replete with fragment of fish, and shredded crab.
May a hundred bowls be set, each clutching a gourmet's delight
in its thick, dark clay, and may each outdo the rest!
Let my courtiers slide in their rich, embroidered silks
and whisper their wicked ambitions up brocaded sleeves.
This dynasty will die with me, which they have guessed,
and even as they sup with me, they plot like thieves.

Old, too old thou art, poor, sad dismembered China!
My wall will not protect thee. It will hold off awhile
barbarians come sniffing out your wealth, and give to kings
come after me a thin white line to hold, by way of border.
But the men of the North will take us, where there is no wall
save that of our own endeavour, a thing of shifting mist.
O ye scholars, who hold me guilty of the murder of your kin:
You will have more vicious kings than me, and all
your defence of the past and settled ways, will be swept
from the board in one savage sweep of the Mongol.

Thus I warn ye, those who still hold their heads,
and nod with them to me in a sycophantic trance.
You have complex made my task, and interrupted policy
with your wise, irreverent fantasies, and worship of the past.
I would have had ye in my gardens, plucking apricots for fruit
of learning, wandering glistening in the sun
and setting off one another, each feeding flame to the rest,
the jewels of my wide and well-respected kingdom.
But you did disappoint me, and did settle to the last
in your puddle of antiquity, and your feudal slum.

Know ye that these ancient, rotting hierarchies
of wealth entrenched and unearnt have had their day.
China is too vast for them, and you with your books
and cunning artifice should know this better than I,
misguided king of half of the earth, with little learning.
My people cry for change, and have a yen for sharing
the fruits of this larder world, whose orchard they tend.
Ought I stifle them, or you? They are so many, and you
but pinpricks on the tapestry of my domains.
I think I have lopped the heads of the dislocated few.

Ah! such a feast for the gods in heaven! The platters spun
of finest stuff, the colours a riot of hue!
And the girls snuck out with their offerings: such exquisite shapes
twisting dim and delicious in transparent silk — ah, to be young
again, and lascivious! I would pick from this crew

of simpering beauties one who would explode tonight
like a firecracker dragon, and drag an emperor
kicking and bucking his majesty's whims to an ecstasy of delight!
As it is, I flick my fingers wearily at the whole menage
and sip at my supper pensively, as an emperor should do.

I have conquered the Huang-nu. Now they will pivot West,
and cursed be the lands they descend upon. Some centuries
will pass before they gather strength, but when it comes
they will pillage all they cross, like a scourge-laden breeze.
People will say: out of China has come a blitz on humanity,
which piles the skulls of our husbands and sons in pyramids.
But these I have swept to the distant North, and sulking there
they will build up their blister of pus, 'til it poisonously burst upon
barbarous folk afar, which will lance the boil, for us.
In a sense, we will win by the trespass of these unholy men.

Except that we shall, saving miracles, be already completely lost
as this flimsy palace of silk and bamboo is torn by the winds.
We sit lazy at our looms, and the freedoms I have won
for my chattering folk, I doubt will survive the storm.
A courtesan, who is paid for this, stretches like a fawn
extending her limbs, and dishes me up a pickle of luscious things.
How my loins ache of this power, and would gather her
in pleasure's mulch, were I not this doddering king.
Her trinkets of jade bob like corks on her foaming breast,
as if she were toy to her emperor, and by him caressed!

The pagoda is built on a lake flecked with colourful weed,
and the pale mist wafts off the water in pastelling swirls.
A fish floats aghast near the surface, lunging at flies,
and a bird sits still in the twisted tree, with expectant eyes.
Like delicate brushings of paint, a clump of bamboo
sways soft in the pink, translucent carpet of dawn.
I sit alone in this watershed, my feast all eaten and gone
and my enemy guests all packed of their hopes, and departed.
My China is spread before me, clogged with the paste and glue
of the systems I have built her, and the tissue of peace I have spun.

Delicatessen, 1971

You seek release from your bulging eyes
and carbuncular face, to eke out the peace
you know lies trapped in the storm of days:

> *ah yes! petals infolded,*
> *resisted time battering;*

> > *the whole palace swimming,*
> > *cascading in roses, yes.*

Or in a rattered delicatessen, eying the flux
of driftwood in and out, a sad procession of pies;
pinned to a laminex table, glued with perspiration,
attempting a sausage roll in this last resort
of plastic pumpkins, cigarettes and lies.

> *We wanted it so much:*
> *it was like white balls exploding,*
> *fanning my face with burning .....*

Hunched upon his sausage,
meat globs dripping
from the corners of his mouth:

> *such a fabulous time ..... Christmas .....*
> *yes, yes ..... Rottnest .....*
> *Emily's meringue was soggy...*
> *We don't have too much time.*
> *There is so   so little time.*

I could love this place with all the black sperm in me
were it not so pert. A thin skein, transparent cupola;
torn sails flapping loose, coagulating failure;
laddered, mismatched stockings; grease stains on your skirt.

> *Perhaps we met in such a place,*
> *perhaps he asked me there*

and I said yes.
My thighs ran like milk
as I swirled cascades of raven hair
down my velvet dress.

Your needs are simpler than mine i.e. money,
placating orgies of hunger, twelve dollars a day.
Your ugliness haunts me — it is almost beauty.
O my pudgy, syrup-eyed girl of the mountains:
come to me smelling of garlic
and I will scavenge.

Song of the Recruiting Officer

It is not for me to query the unquestionable:
Who it is who governs, who ordains the timetable
Of ritual and experience, who organises lists
Of drab statistic. Not for me to question.

I have stood in row-of-four, seen damper fists
Than mine in moist salute, wandered
Past lines of raw recruits drawn up for inspection.
I have led the routine of obedience, squandered
My life so far in simply sterilising infection.

Words lie, unheard, and those that are thought
Get their just reward. Nature does not really care
If some of its spawn seeks defection.
No, take a good wine, settle in the observation car
For the journey. Every eater must shoot his share.
The secret is to escape detection.

An Ode to Pisces (Whose Day has Ended)

We are told that the Age of Pisces, which apparently, due to a specific conglomeration of planets, has held sway for some two thousand years, gave way, on Friday 12th January, 1996, to the Age of Aquarius, which will, courtesy of the planet Uranus, rule us for the next two thousand or so years. Assuming that we are to some extent, like the tides of the sea and our very bodies, affected by such things (which theory scientists, of course, reject vociferously - but who has ever taken any notice of them?), then the ushering in of this new cosmic order might lend some hope that the rather depressing antics of humanity in the last two millennia might be bettered in the next. The Author is of the view, however, that the Age of Pisces, with all its baggage of religious fervour, horrid wars, and strangely vindictive pestilence, should not be allowed to pass without even a whimper of a requiem, which the following is designed to provide. R.I.P., if that is possible, thou terrifying and terrible age, and may never such a one come again to haunt this fragile world, and fill its dreams with such demons.

I

The soul aches, as another century
  Draws blindly on towards its gloomy close.
An age, too, is ending. There seems to be
  A freshness in the wind, the scent of those
Who are children still in an old and decrepit world.
  Die, thou Pisces! For two thousand years
    Your agony was hung upon the cross
    And to dark pits hurled.
  Of flesh has been thy bread, and your chalice of tears
    Has been squeezed from the ducts of misery and loss.

II

Your cathedrals are empty now, except for the swill
  Of flashbulb tourists, peering at time-worn rock.
Your vergers dodder aimless, chattering still
  Of the glories of God and his minions, and his dwindling flock.
In stone has been etched your beauty, and it is intense
  In its sharp relief of pain. Your hovering hymns,
    Like the cries of the damned, lend an evil and desperate din
      To your liturgy clotted and dense.
  Yours was the age of the devil, and your slimy sins
    Are worse for the velvet stole you have cloaked them in.

III

Your marshals have had their day, and been lain to rest
  In the horrid clamour of pomp, and alarums of brass.
Birds drop turds on their monuments. Their quest
  To be king of the killing fields is ended at last.
Duller men have replaced them, and kings wear ties
  As they broker peace to their subjects, and flinch at war.
    There is hope lurking in corners, and a sense of shock
      Greets politicians' lies.
    Your children have turned their backs on you, and your
      Crumbling house. They will build it anew, but on rock.

IV

Some lived too early, and were trapped in your inky sea:
  Marcus Aurelius, prince of civilised thought.
Socrates, who would rather die than see
  The crowning of Untruth, and its gibbering court.
Erasmus, dear, quaint soul, who hated so
  Foul Luther's gobbling God, glaring above.
    Rabelais, who'd make a wall of cunts
      To foil invaders, and to slow
The rape of Paris with this trembling lure of love.
  Chaucer, who taught us that we live but once,

V

And that laughter be all travail's spice and hue.
  Jane Austen, wry and obedient vicar's miss
Whose affection wrestled with wisdom, but whose thrust cut true.
  Dickens, who did hate you, Pisces, and whose hiss
At your hypocrisy was windy blight to thee.
  These, your changeling spawn, made mock of you,
    And your gaping splendour, and bubbling, poisonous breath.
    They hold the victory
  Over all you've done, and still would wickedly do.
    Their song is a barcarole to your lingering death.

VI

And now comes a swarm of children across frozen earth,
  Singing and tumbling and laughing in quick surprise.
Their hair is tangled unkempt, and in spite of their mirth
  Dark shadows lurk in the twinkling pools of their eyes.
They are led by a blind old vicar, stumbling along,
  Mumbling out his homilies like a cackling crow.
    These are the last-born of Pisces, and the last
      Who will hear your mournful song.
  They'll inherit this swampy place, and will come to know
    In the chill of their bones its icy winter blast.

VII

They will delve their gardens deep but to open graves.
  This history we leave them is thick with the stench of blood.
The earth that they till will be poisonous bad, and as slaves
  To their terrible past they will toil in this cauldron of mud.
These, then, are the Aquarians, to whom we leave
  Our life-forms, sick to their gills, and green with disease;
    Some listing monuments, and a feast of tombs,
      That they learn how to wail and grieve.
  Mad misers that we are, afeared our legacies
    Might somehow rob us yet, in our catacombs.

VIII

Adieu, sad age! (If that He'll take you in,
  Or recognise your tiny, worthless prayer).
The eastern sky is flecked with gold and tin
  And the sun is climbing purple through the air.
A flute is drowning out your drums of war
  And a shimmer of beauty rises like a mist.
    A scent of apple blossom makes the senses run
      To thrill me to the core.
  A child is born, which your palsied lips have kissed
    All fruitlessly, since your savage rule is done.

A Letter Home

for Adam Lindsay Gordon

Here's a'hoping you'll receive this tattered letter, Mary,
which I'm writing in my shanty, near my mine.
They're neither very big ones, but they're all I've got to show
for three long, suffering years. There's a glow
above the goldfields, the moon's soft, silky shine
sprinkled like the teardrops of a fairy.

I love you dear, sweet sour-puss, my Mary.
I'd drink thee deep, if I had any wine.
The old Hurricane is spluttery — its wick's begun to go,
or this dervish wind too strong, or the oil too low.
I can scarcely read these spider words of mine
which twitch across this page so spindly hairy.

How's dear old London town, my merry Mary?
Do the barrow-boys still croon their cheeky whine?
The dull old river run, sedate and slick and slow
and the barges loom like monsters through the snow?
Does it drizzle there, as ever, and the fog still wind
itself in crazy shapes, what used to scare thee?

Here it's hot as you would never guess, cool Mary,
and the days are long in the belly of my mine.
I've a break in the afternoon, when I chew my dumpling dough
and the sweat cakes salt on my shoulder-blades. I know
I'll strike it lucky soon, and in certain time
prise from the earth rich gilden-craft to bear thee.

In the letter that you latest sent me, Mary,
I sensed a certain distance in your mind.
It's been a dreary wait, poor lass, and the gold sneaks slow
from the rotten, clotted clay of Bendigo.
In London there's exciting fare, and a line
of well-dressed toffs to bedevil, and to snare thee.

My Miner's Right gives me this little patch, Mary,
to hew and hack the fortune that is mine.
It does not cross the seas, nor hold you in escrow
to my rattly shovel and pick. You are free to go
where you wilt in life, and with him you want for thine.
I will dig with my feverish hope, but I will not swear thee.

That's a kookaburra laughing, my dear Mary,
a queer, puffy bird what scoffs at Time.
This vast, drear land is strange — 'twould give thee vertigo
at its very docks. Yet it makes a giddy show
of splendour mixed with terror, a tangled vine
of grape and gravelstone, to delight and despair thee.

The diggings are spread for forty miles, Mary,
and the tents yawn higgledy-piggledy down the line.
There's a mess of humanity here, with nowhere else to go
but down in the earth like moles, with their eyes aglow.
All have equal fortune, and each his minuscule mine
to fossick in, and be lord of. Ah, you'd be chary

worse than of foggy shapes, my puddling Mary,
to be thick with this muddle o' men in the heat o' their wine!
They are rough and greedy dwarves, their wits besotted and slow
in their own defence, as their fortunes gather and go.
They will never be rich as me, whose glittering mine
is moist and soft in London, and is waiting for me.

Or so I hope, and trust, and pray, my darling Mary,
if thou can'st keep our flame of love alive.
I will claw from this hostile earth the treasures that I owe,
and return like a Viking bold with my hoard in tow,
but aware that the cloth of gold that was ever mine
was ever there, had I noticed, rigged all a-square ye.

For Margaret Parker

for my Mother-in-law, renowned Jumble-Saler and fossicker, about to head back West, after staying with us in the Blue Mountains for a period.

You have been with us now, old Margaret Jarley, several weeks
and merry have been our boisterings, in that short time.
Well jumbled we have, up and down the mountains' mist,
in hunt of the gold which fools cast aimlessly aside:
their beady pearls, exotic books, and former pride.
You have brought laughter to us, and made shake our cheeks
with absurd amusement. For this we thank you in simple rhyme,
and reverently, for the chalice of joy you have held us to kiss.

You have made poor mess of us at Scrabble, and the pearls you cast
on our doubting, dictionary ways have ungrammared us.
Some of these were suspect, but you hustled us to wit
and bright new words, whose worth lay buried deep in the dark.
In fact, you have helped us re-define language, albeit a stark
and idiotic tongue which is not English, and will not last.
But it is you, and your scrabbly way, and your "antrobus"
scores 46 on any scale, whether triple-scored or not.

You grow old, and fear that in doing so you might trigger
fear in others' hearts, that they might be stuck with you.
Fear not, old dame of slurping merriment. You are secure
in all our love of all that lives and laughs and sings
and makes of life a smorgasbord. Let us live like kings
and queens and princesses henceforth, and let not the snigger
of the surly knave sneak upon our pack. Soft dew
sits young and sweet upon your years, and may it endure.

So gather up thy whitened hairs (with copper hints)
and bend thyself to Perth. But do not tarry long
in that sad swamp. Pack up thy bricken bracken, and books,
and get thee back to where your wax-works can take roost.
The audience to your caravan will be small, and at best
will number up your family, in all its garish tints.
You are much loved by all of these, and should feel strong
in their gruff embrace, and mumbled plans, and muddled looks.

A Winter's Taylor

On hearing that Mr Rod Moran's collection of verse "Listening to the Train Passing" had been outvoted (in a short-list of two) for the WA Premier's Literary Award by an inane collection of trivia produced by Professor Andrew Taylor, a minor and irritatingly ingratiating talent we had all rather written off to the area of pleasantries upon the subject of his baby daughter, the woes of attempting to teach, and other such salutary subjects wherein he speaks with authority.

Rod, when yer old, and sick, and stupid, and yer versifyin's done,
and yer wonder why yer bothered with yer pomes an' shit and stuff,
When yer puzzle where the money ain't, and yer Poet's race is run,
then just tear yer fucking ticket up, and call: "Enuff's enuff!"

I've read me fill of Poetry, I've read me fill of yours,
I've read this new bloke Taylor's gear, and heard him spout his guff.
I've listened to the best and worst, the wherefore and because,
and shit! I'd back me Aunty Jean to author better stuff!

His bawling bloody baby! Shit, I'd fling it to the wolves,
or dingoes maybe, anything, to get it off the map!
Who gives a fuck about his seedy, replicating tools
or wretched wife left languishing while he's at arty yap?

Nah, up his twot! That's where his poems comes from.
And now this prize, thin thing carved out of turds.
He has emasculated verse — no, worse, he has let come
upon our sacred grove an insecticide of words

which shrivels flower and fern, and all our little plot,
our leafy laughter, joy of words, and arbitrage of skill.
He is antithesis of art, a veritable blot
on our gilden-graft of garden, a piss-pot of ill.

So fuck him sideways! Miserable nerd
on $80k, but hungry still for more.
His stomach heaves for notice, howso grotesque and absurd
his posturings, his purposes are sure,

which are: to place himself at the head of the withered tree
that never will bear leaf nor fruit, nor spread its shade,
alone in his sticky kingdom, a disorientated bee
carved off its hive, and honey-dreams, and flower-glade.

And I say: yer've gotter reckon that this all is fair enough!
This is Poertry terday, cain't yer see what's plain ter see?
They just don't want yer beauty, or yer sweetly scanning stuff,
They want their cosy little club, and no derogatory.

So when yer old, and sick, and stupid, and yer versifyin's stuck,
and yer wonder why yer bothered with yer pomes and verbal spews,
y'cn haul out Andrew Taylor's slim-vol prize-awarded muck,
and be glad yer not the winner in a race of cockatoos.

The Banker and the Bird

"Why do you slide along on your belly?" asked the Magpie of the Snail.
"Do you have no sense of ribaldry, nor idle fun?
Are you quite content to hump in your shell, hunch head into tail
and mooch about like a banker, safe, but glum?"

"That's all very well for you," said the Snail with a bitter grin,
"as you waft about in the heavens, and perch in your trees.
You own not a scrap of property, nor one single thing
to sustain your random path on the fidgeting breeze."

"That's true, I suppose," said the Magpie, "though it's cautious wit.
You could say I'm a flippant feller, and careless as sin.
I've nothing left from yesterday but the memory of it,
but there's interest in that, I can tell you, and a capital thing!"

"Bah! Look at me," said the Snail, "I've a house to my back,
a position in life, though a small one, and a slow-filling cup.
I'm even considering......" But with terrible flutter and crack
the Magpie swooped down from its branches, and gobbled him up.

Di Provenza il mar

Germont's great aria from Verdi's troubled masterpiece La Traviata *will touch off a chord in all fathers' hearts, as I'm sure Verdi intended. Not even he, however, would have anticipated that someday a second genius in the shape of Tito Gobbi would front up to render it. He who does not weep at this exotic combination has never had a daughter, or else has never lived. For my step-daughter Emma.*

Come back with me, my little dove
who pecked at me when that thou wert young.
Frail, frightened thing. O that my love
might feather thee up with its fluffy song!

What a mess we did in raising thee.
Filled thy head with fancy, and a sense
that all you did were sacrosanct. And merrily
you rose to this, like a fish to the scent

of artful bait, and the flash of the fly.
My poor, indulged and doting daughter,
how we guddled you, and let drift by
your training of the pond, and of fishy slaughter.

Now you gape at the world as if plucked from the water
what cloaked you in. You are so young
to be jerked into air, with the line drawn tauter
and slicing about you, and your death-song sung.

But 'tis bird thou art, not fish, little fledgling,
though thy wings be damp and thick with the sea,
and beating on the wind, you'll wing
upwards to the sun, and back towards me.

Back to where sickness cannot be,
where we used to live. Your mother, there,
will dispense the balm of her love sweetly
through her fingers, as she fondles your hair.

Ah, come back, come back, my speckled thing!
This world is but throttled lung for thee,
and all its adventure but a venturing
to careering lust, and cruelty.

At home the vine sags sweaty and hot,
and the smell of bread hangs fresh in the air.
Your herbs grow lank in abandoned plot,
and the roses droop that you are not there,

whilst our scattered garden seems but a bare
and withered thing, all riddled with weeds
and neglect, a burden of heavy care.
Provence cries out for you, and grieves

for thee, as do we, my little dove,
who breasted thee when that thou wert young.
Return, my darling, to that nest of love
from which you were idly, foolishly flung.

A letter from Helen

On her seventy-fifth birthday (June, 1996) my mother, Helen, sent me
the following short poem.

> *Three quarters of a century ago*
> *I opened wide my eyes and took first breath.*
> *My father, loving man, penned thus to me*
> *In later years. To me, his first born child.*
>
>> 'Tis fifteen years ago today
>> Or will be when you get this letter,
>> That true to type you came along
>> In time to hear the dinner gong,
>> And all the birds burst into song
>> Because they felt the world was better.
>
> *And that is sixty years' past! It seems*
> *Incredible to me who feels not mild,*

As would befit my years, but strong
And young enough to tackle life — its woes
Or joys. To fight, to float serene; who dreams
E'en yet of winning through to higher ground
From whence I can survey my conquered foes.
Friends and foes and lovers all combined
In making life a wondrous pilgrimage;
Selflessness and ecstasy and rage
Extended the horizons of my mind.
Three quarters of a century ago
I opened wide my eyes and took first breath.
I have loved life, and angry shall I go
To that last battle, with the victor death.

A letter back

for Helen, turned seventy five

Yes angry go, old dame, on that last pilgrimage
to that grim cathedral where they preach of naught but death.
As the child grows wild and uncontrollable with rage
when the day of her petty party pride draws final breath;

and cross and grumpy is she hauled to her lonely bed
above the chatter and muffled joy of the lingering guest,
and lies there like a porcupine, with a bristling head
of spiked aggression curled upon her clenched breast,

and even then, though night has come, and she is cast
to unspeakable dark where none can play or fight or fend,
plots out the small but terrible plans, which to her seem vast
reprisal on her enemies, and her bleak revenge.

And angry be, venerable Dame, that at this last
oasis of peace and joy thou hast delightfully found
there should still sit gremlins grinning, and vultures winging fast
above thee, as they eye thee off, and hover round.

Let anger settle doubly on the envious fools
and pimps and charlatans who have taken of thy wealth
'til purse thou had no more, who have sucked dry the pools
of life and laughter bubbling up, and thy liquid health.

You say you have loved your life — but you also have been loved.
There's those who will bear thee gold, and frankincense, and myrrh.
Those you've cradled with care, and fondled dear, and proved
a force beyond reason or need which gleams like a mighty star

through the black thickets of mist which bedevil the wandering ones
who seek a person or thing they might bow to in love and remorse.
Your son born without prospect of speech, indeed both your sons
whom you fussed, and rescued from pain, as a matter of course.

And your daughters, who fight and nag, and horribly bicker and curse
but whose memory is keen when it comes to the matters which tell.
Those you have succoured and fed need not practise nor rehearse
their feelings in such matters. Like a strong and sturdy bell

which peals across the desert sands from some monastery
comes your cry of angry joy as you grip and cling to life,
and those who have nestled there, on this journey's mystery,
remember well its leafy walks, and its walls against strife.

And like the fading frescoes of that cool, refreshing place
are the templates of lives you have led, and are yet to lead.
There is no death in such old halls, which are decked with a grace
no human hand could tint, nor architect conceive.

No death, but a wilting out into long refreshing sleep,
like the child you wilfully are, and have ever been.
But the bedlamp flickers yet, and there is no cause to weep
too soon the passing of day into night's unending dream.

See the shadows on the roof! How they caper and wobble and flit!
Feel the rich dark quilt of night as it hovers and cloaks you in!
The party below is but scattered cakes — you are be-shot of it
in this ecstasy of yourself at last, old Bedouin!

Ter Mister Oakley

for Barry Oakley, who wrote wonderingly of us mountain-folk in his
newspaper column, and then sidled up towards us, as far as Glenbrook at
least. Which is not really mountains as such, but foothill. Mr Oakley had
expressed a certain derision at our mountain ways, and accused us of
offering a sort of lofty sleight of hand towards our brethren of the plain,
particularly in the matter of real estate, and the much-touted dream
hideaways of these regions, which give over so often to nightmare.

So yer've come up ter the mountains, Mr Oakley,
and I 'spect yer feeling pretty bloody smug.
Even though its only Glenbrook, just a hillock in the scrub,
yer can caper in yer funny hat, all quaint and folkly,

Mr Oakley. Yeah, we're funny folk up here,
not like yer Balmain mob, nor bleedin' poets.
Y'could say we live a lonely life; y'could sneer
at our snuffling ways, and our eerie habits.

Aw, I'm sure you'll scoff at this. I read yer stuff
in the coloured picture magerzine what comes with the paper.
Y'thought us pretty hill-billy — well, fair enough:
we've hills to burn, and potter in, and caper.

Yeah, Balmain. I went there once, and feared fer me bum
as I strode the sidewalk cafes tryin' ter look quaint.
But me mountain ways undid me: I couldn't help but hum
Slim Dusty numbers, which fashion *there* it ain't.

Nah, they giggled at me, and not only just the girls.
I felt like a prick in a footy sock, erect to no use.
In fact I was glad to get back to my wrinkled hills
where the mist clamps you in, and the clothes you wear hang loose.

Ah yes, in Katoomba. To my weatherboard shack near the cliff
where the clean mountain air saws at yer lungs like a knife.
Where a Drizabone counts as evening gear, and the wonder is if
Y'should wear aught else to dinner, or when humping yer wife,

assuming yer do so, which yer may or may not. Up here
we're discursive on this, since our wives are rangy and lean.
Bein' mountain girls, they have their own slightly queer
ways of pleasin' their men. They can get mean

and cantankerous, and they blatantly dislike writers.
'Course, no dart at yerself. Can't help what yer do.
Have yer thort of joining St Vinnie de Pauls, or the Fire-fighters?
Dont'cha worry. They'll think of something Mountainous fer you

down Glenbrook way, ter fill up yer time. They always do.
'Course, they'll leave you alone at first. You'll just be
the newest beard in town. They'll bob and duck to you
fer a bit, in the *paper* and all, with all the mystery

that attends such pulpy fame. But that will soon sink
in the mountain muck that comes gurgling out of the turf.
They'll be watching you, to see if the Balmain stink
still hangs about your kitchen like a sickly curse.

Which it will, you know. You cannot come up here
like some acolyte who seeks the guru's lichened groves,
mumbling into yer whiskers as you seek yer perfumed seer
who can put Balmain behind yer, with a tilt of his nose.

Nah, Barry, get real. Glenbrook! Shit:
It ain't even real mountain. It's like Thomas Mann
cut in half and half again, or a Jesuit
taught a third of his craft, or a rug half-spun.

So yer reckon yer c'n *breathe* again down there!
Well, that's something. Poets, I hear, are dying
cockroach-thick down Darling Street for lack of air.
I have heard that the Balmain publicans are sighing

fer the good old days, when writers had brains and money,
and when artists sucked beer, not smack. Perhaps it is this
which has driven you lemming-like westwards, though up. Funny
you should buzz from one trap to another, though, in your exodus.

For the mountain, even though on its slopes, will patina you
and your Oakley tribe with its thick and terrible skin.
Never more may you smoke in a restaurant, nor dare to hew
a tree above 3.9 metres which is cloying you in;

Nor will you ever again be free to express
an un-mountainous view, or one which endeavours to tell
of a life beyond kit-homes of cedar, or the Mountains Gazette,
or the Blue Mountains Council which now is your guide through
      the scrublands of hell.

And never again must you raise, in the shit-Sydney press
the spectre of mountain angst, as you recently dared.
Or sneer at the real estate here, in a bid to impress
your womenfolk with your city *savoir faire*.

The mountains have beckoned to many — yes, writers, too.
Each wave of such brainy types they have sucked within,
and gurgling softly, have digested all this brew
with plopping burp and leafy belch and stupid grin.

Here people come to die, at a decent height.
They do not need your sneering at their nooks.
Nor do they share your pity at their plight
or their shuttering, as they hang upon their hooks.

You will learn that mountain folk are crazily content
as they gaze upon the city of the plain.
Their restaurants may be foul, and their one intent
survival of the frost. But again and again

they drive their rhododendrons in an arc towards the sky,
and coo to their elms and birches in a most un-Australian display.
They are mad, of course, these lofty *lotophagoi*
you have crept amongst. But welcome, anyway.

Rommel, to his wife

My darling, as I think on you, I sit aloft
these tilting Libyan sands, and write you this.
This war is all undone, and my part in it
unravelled like a spindle, idly flung.

I have batoned out my relay here: ay, and nobly run.
Success we have drunk, and the thin kerosene of defeat.
The sand crawls about us, as it has ever done
round the wandering tribes that jostle here, and jousting meet.

Ah, what a wretched, futile, gnomic thing it is, this war,
this to and fro in the desert, this trance of death.
I am here as its commander, but, love, it orders me
to my daily, dutiful march toward hideousness.

And all to serve that strutting loon you hold at home
as if he were some icon, or some flaming star
set high in the heavens to agitate and cozen us
across this arid earth to Bethlehem.

Around me die my sleek young men, like lobsters cooked
in the steaming tubs of their tanks, in the furnace dipped.
Black crisps when we yank them out with our rescuing hooks.
Just powder to place in this hot red earth we are captured in.

I have no idea why I order them forward, then back in retreat,
then forward again, to flourish our conquering cry.
I follow my skill, which is mighty, without knowing if
I am serving a god or a monster. Or, in either case, why.

Monty will beat us, of course. He has petrol, which we do not.
He has shells to his breech, and an endless source of supply.
We are fossickers merely, like moths dropped in the pot,
and like all such scavenging pests, we deserve to die.

> *So kiss this letter, my darling, before it is tossed*
> *to the bleak and cheerless fire. This war, this life, is lost.*

Envoi

for all my friends and enemies, who form up but one small cell together

Go, little book, like plankton,
skimming across the ocean of our pleasures;
Go whisper them
who, hung in a lonely hammock, or huddled in spidery nook
swing upon feathery, fragile threads
and hum to their very selves the hymn of bitterness,
and cuddle hatred, like a hook.
Go counsel them, go succour them.

Reveal, if you can, a chink into the treasures
fast in Ali Baba's cave, roll back the rock
that keeps them hence, shout *Open Sesame*!
and open up their ears to that giggling mob of thieves
who've hopped into oily pots,
and smeared their grimy snot down patchwork sleeves.

O little book, spin thou thy plots
and thy sticky webs, thy coarse magic weave
in the cave of all our longing, all our care!
Help us become as children once again,
with eyes alight like fireflies!
Let limbs jerk like crazy toys
teased into living, let our weighty minds
turn helium, or like the breath of chattering girls and boys
puff out in a quick quirk: o, let your songs bring
the very stuff of living back into every adult thing!

Thou book, such a stiff task to give you.
Art but pages, smelly ink, dull printed thing.
Can'st bear this burden, or this sharp refrain?
Thou art clever and ingenious, but can'st thou thus-fold sing?
Can'st thrill our sharp endeavour, and resuscitate again
that tilt of liquid living, or rejuvenate that flame
dwindled to an ember, sunk in the ash of all our years?
Can'st re-ignite our laughter, and so sizzle up our tears?

Poor book, to set for thee such hurdles,
when all thou wanted was to leap and sing!
Forget these strict instructions — go skittering
where'er thou wilt, poke ribald tongue
at prudent prudes, and cautious men,
and tug what skirts excite thy nimble lust,
thou leprechaun!

But be thou ever gentle in thy gambols — needs must
be generous, e'en as thou mock, and mak'st to-do.
Do not sneer altogether, for thou must understand
what tiny drop thou art in life's great swell,
how small a thing thou art, how young, and new.
Perhaps you grasp the sun in a passing moment,
and sparkle briefly, but that is all you do.

So, book, go shimmer in thy currents,
and skip 'cross froth, and spin in the shivering air,
and where you fuse with elemental torrents
with weed, and wave, and shell dragged everywhere,
then let your little strictures softly wetten,
and all your pompous wisdom flatten in,
and when your tiny song is all forgotten,
make coral caves to resonate some other's din.

Small scuttling creature, octopus of verse.
I let thee loose, to set about thy work.
Seems such little labour, now, like child's play:
Book, thou must wreak us tiny spells,
to out-children children, and must carry us back,
if you can, to a time before time, when we were but shiny cells
adrift in the ocean. Ah, what we might have become!

Tall order, book. In fact, too much for you,
and your faltering, scrupulous song.
Go frighten dames, and screech at the righteous and godly.
Do what thou wilt! Thou art freed of my devil's prong.

Songs from the plays

'Birinski's Song' is from my play *An Ordinary Man*, written in 1986. Birinski, a character therein, is a rather disreputable Russian Jew, and sings this song in a tavern early on in the piece.

'Child in the Forest' is written as a song to be sung by The Railway Inspector in my play *The Commander of Kalda*, performed in Perth by The Winter Theatre Company in 1984. The play is based upon a short-story fragment of Kafka's diaries, wherein the somewhat haunting first line of this poem is to be found.

Molly's two songs are from a planned 'colonial' musical piece along the lines of *The Beggar's Opera*.

I wrote the musical or opera libretto *The Goliards* in 1995, and the following contains a substantial selection of the songs from the piece.

These songs are all, of course, intended to be set to music and sung, either as solo arias, or as duets, trios, quartets etc. The drama is set in Paris of the twelfth century, and has as its central characters two wandering goliards (Eberhard and Michael).

The goliards were vagrant poets and songsters — usually unbeneficed clerks or young ordained men with a certain amount of learning and study behind them, but no real prospects of making an ordinary living. They must have been great pests, though probably thoroughly delightful ones in the main.

The other principal character of the piece is Peter Abelard, famous for his love affair with Heloise (who does not appear in this play, since it is set when they are both old, long separated, and close to Abelard's death). I have invented a daughter for Abelard and Heloise, called Elise, who only discovers this relationship towards the end of the piece.

Other of the songs are various drinking songs by the students at the tavern frequented by the goliards (which is run by an old dwarf, Erda), a scurrilous ditty sung by a rakish Bishop with the goliards and His Eminence's ghastly assistant Hortensio, and a song by the goliards with some passing troupsters (Freak and his little maid Thistledown) who are about to mount their play at the fair in Paris.

The piece is a tolerably cheerful one, but is not, I'm afraid, wholly accurate in every historical detail, and is thus not altogether likely to impress every scholar of the period.

Still, it wasn't written for them.

Birinski's Song

The sun comes up on Moscow town
From the grip of a distant sea,
The sun winks out, and the sun beats down,
And the sun cuts loose with a red-hot frown,
But it does not burn for me.

The sun has scattered all the frost
and frozen memory,
All of the winter's gains are lost
Ice and sludge and sleet are tossed
like waves on a sunlit sea.

And a sailor's mind turns back to his ropes
and the endless churn of lee,
But I grow cold as the sun grows warm
And I shiver with fear in the sun's rich swarm
which sheds no heat on me.

For I and mine have none of it,
this sun, and its sparkling sea.
Our lives are as thin as candle-light
flickering tapers in the night
which burn so fitfully.

So quick, so quick the light is shed,
and fled from you and me.
Deep are the waters where we were bred,
Dark, dark the living dead
in that rolling human sea.

The sun comes up on Moscow town
From the icy grip of the sea,
The sun winks out, and the sun beats down,
And the sun cuts loose with a red-hot frown,
But it does not burn for me.

Child in the Forest

Where are you going, o child in the forest;
What path are you winding, child of mine?
Is it a moss green dream to tomorrow,
Scented with lavender, violet and thyme?

Or is it the bristle of innocent terror,
Lost in this tangle of creeper and vine?
Why do your eyes, which are hooded in sorrow
Shiver in mirrors this fear of mine?

Your pale white legs are all twisted with torture,
Your lips are all thick, and bloated with slime;
What have they done to the creature we nurtured,
Longed for and loved for, and hoarded our time?

Where are you going, o child in the forest,
dreading each step into mysteries of time?
Where is the laughter we carelessly flourished,
Blending the dregs of our squandered wine?

Molly's First Song

1830, London

CHORUS: *Give us a man, girls, any old man,*
                 Let him have balls, girls, any old type;
                 And a fat, bulging wallet, that's what we like.
                 Give us a man, girls, here's to the men!

I once took a boy, girls, in old London Town,
And he hardly suspected he'd met up with vice,
His cheeks were aglow with the softest of down,
Prettier than sin, girls, and ten times as nice.

CHORUS: *Give us a man, girls, any old man etc.*

And he was as pure as a fish in the stream,
with hardly a clue about everyman's curse;
Through all the black night I frothed with his cream
as my shivering fingers emptied his purse.

CHORUS: *Give us a man, girls, any old man etc.*

And when he was done he was full of his sorrow,
Sat on my bed all wet with his woe;
For love dies hard on the heels of tomorrow,
When the sun makes you stumble, pay up, and go.

CHORUS: *Give us a man, girls, any old man etc.*

Later my Arnie came in for the booty,
Four winking gold sovereigns we'd plucked from his crotch;
But strange to relate, girls, this derelict duty:
Because of his sobbing I'd left him his watch.

CHORUS: *Give us a man, girls, any old man etc.*

Now you know I'll have any, that goes without saying,
For the green London slut has no other life;
but sometimes I spit at these drunkards a-laying,
And think of my herring, who wanted to wife.

Molly's Second Song

c. 1850, Hawkesbury River

Now a man is a noble and wonderful thing
When his purse is as fat as his paw;
I've a love for his money, and spending's a joy
But always I'm hungry for more.

And a man can't be bettered if he cares for his wife,
Keeps poverty far from her door;
But at times you get lonely all smothered with love
And you get kinda hungry for more.

The ones who are handsome are scarce, it is true,
In their eyes a woman's a whore.
They'll feed you sweet honey and rich caviar
But you'll feel sorta peckish for more.

There's men who'll not heed you, nor look at you twice,
And you'll pound late at night on their door.
They'll sneer in your face as they slump off to bed
And you're left pretty desperate for more.

There are men fit to cheat you, men fit to beat you
And men who you'd love 'til you're sore.
But the man isn't made who'll make love in the grave
Which is why I'm so anxious for more.

One day he'll appear, that man of your dreams,
Rich man and lover and more.
He'll blaze like the sun 'til the night blots him out
And you're hungrier now than before.

I'm a woman, a lover, the giver of life,
I'm a feast to be spread on the floor.
I'm a mother, a daughter, and twenty times wife,
But my belly still rumbles for more.

Songs from The Goliards

The Goliards' Song

As the sun lifts tousled head
And shrugs his care, and sleep away
And hoists him up from his dark bed
So rises up the goliard

And as the sky is his wide way
Through heaven's gates his path ahead
He bathes the world in brilliant day
and lights upon the goliard

Proud goliard, gay goliard!
Love's careless toy, life's gift of song
Let all the world sing loud and long
the praises of the goliard!

A sleepy maid lifts pretty head
to hear soft note, so sweetly sung
Smoothes the feathers round her bed
and whispers to the goliard

The cock hath crown, its lusty lung
Has filled the town, and warmed the dead
Grim merchants smile, sad priests are wrung
to pleasure's hymn, by goliard

Proud goliard, gay goliard!
Thou set'st the stars about the sun
Night's necklace thou hast caused to run
To liquid gold, thou goliard

Proud goliard, gay goliard!
The world doth melt in thy hot song
The cold are warmed, the weak grown strong
by passing of the goliard

Eberhard's Song

Spent and gone, my every farthing
washed away, my careless hoard
What little left, was lent to others
So with my song, I beg my board

My coins were few, and were but copper
My purse is thin, and sucks its sides
I was not born to swollen fortune
My wealth is art, and there resides

Spring is burst from miser Winter
Robin Red-breast puffs and skites
His piping flute's not played for treasure
But for the joy which he excites

For thee I'll sing, and that right sweetly
For thee I'll spend, for thee I'll pine
Your shining face will pay me neatly
All the coin I'd take for mine

For here is peace, and love and pleasure
Here your bills are paid in kind
Your simple feast is shared at leisure
Sprinkled o'er with heaven's wine

Trio (Goliards and Elise)

EBERHARD   My song is all, 'tis is all I have
                     'tis all my wisdom, all my wealth
                     all my strength, and all my sorrow
                     all desire, and all my health

ELISE   You warble sweet, you strange young man
                     frail feathered thing, with throat so strong
                     The nightingale perched in thy hand
                     spills out his stream of silver song

MICHAEL	Keep far from here, you foolish maid This garden's fruit is not for thee Beneath that song lies heart of stone and in its coldness, misery
EBERHARD	I'll sing again, for love comes creeping Stealing o'er this barren plain Dream thou of me, while softly sleeping and fetch away my lonely pain
ELISE	I'll dream of all that's sweet and lovely the mystery of God's generous grace Your ragged looks, and gait ungainly Your mad great eyes, your gentle face
MICHAEL	The night will fill with thin hobgoblins 'ere it's done, you'll rue their spite No troubadour knows love's sweet trouble beyond the charms he can excite
EBERHARD	I'll spread my wings, to test their carriage and fly with thee, in heaven's face Love's soaring song will seal a marriage girded round with clouds of lace
ELISE	We'll fly as one, my sweet young sparrow 'til specks we seem to every eye Cross heaven's field, we'll lay a harrow and build a meadow in the sky
EBERHARD	And when at last we fall exhausted and the earth receives us in the love we've shared, and joy we've fostered will feather o'er our tiny sin

Eberhard's Lament

How cruel is love, o cruelty!
And cruel is God, who leaves me free
To squander love so fruitlessly
The blossoms wilting on the tree
make love's bouquet a mockery

What fool is love, o trickery!
And fool is God, who feeds to me
the rotten fruit from his twisted tree
My laughter thins to a bitter glee
at such queer delight, that clowns with me

How cruel is love, o cruelty!
How cruel is life's sad mystery!
We share but our pain, and our misery
The blight which sucks at the root of the tree
is all my love, so cruel to me

Students' Tavern Song

CHORUS   Wine is our blood, rich red our wine
               We hang our cups on the One True Cross
               What's mine is yours, what's yours is mine
               Let's muddle up our bellies! Come, heads back, toss!

ERDA   *Come set ye down, ye drunken goons*
               Come slurp your beer, and suck your pot
               Life's young fools, come bang your spoons
               Spew up the wisdom you've forgot!

CHORUS   Come start your drinking
               slinking, winking
               fill your goblet, fill your pot!
               Sluggard, rugged
               be-slippered or be-buggered
               up from your slime-pit, up from your cot!

Come drink with us!
If you can, if you dare
we'll drink until we slump
in the corner there
though the beer be made of pus!
and the wine is gathered up
from the virgin's bloody cunt

Come drink with us:
    In vino veritas!

Come start your drinking
shrinking, stinking
always drinking
never mind your thinking
think about your drinking
drink all life's cup!
Let women's pretty labials
form up thy goblet's rim!
Thy drinking feats be fabled
in every riotous inn!

Come drink with us:
    In vino veritas!

ERDA   *Ay, drink 'til the rafters fall from the ceiling*
    drink 'til thy heads sag about like a sock!
    drink up thy wits, and drink away thy feeling
    drink up thy youth, drink until you rot!

ALL   Always drinking
    drinking 'til we're shrinking
    drinking 'til we're reeling like a drunken sot!
    Always drinking
    obliterating thinking
    drinking 'til we're raving like an Ostrogoth!

GRIMKIN   *Let no woman near*
this holy rite
she will hiss and rear
and she'll scratch and bite

For she'll never understand
what mystery drives us on to drink and sing
She likes a sober man
to run about the house and fetch her things ......

ALL   Whilst we want drinking
ever to be drinking
we'll slosh away and wash away this female blight!
no matter if we're slinking
vomiting and stinking
men will have their bottle in the middle o' the night!

Come drink with us
if you can, if you dare
We'll drink until we slump
in the corner there
though the world will rail at us
and drench us with disgust
so to liquidate our lust

Come drink with us:
    In vino veritas!

Abelard and Elise

ABELARD

O daughter who is free of sin
Yet must confess
Thou art an angel
In mortal dress
Your crimes breed pity
in this sunken breast
Thou can'st not sin
Yet thou must confess

ELISE

I have sinned
and I must confess
My thought flows hot
through my soul's distress
I would cool my head
on thy gentle breast
O Saviour dear
I must confess

ABELARD

If love is sin
then thou must confess
And so must God
and His choirs of the blessed
What stole shall we choose
in what garb will we dress
when He whispers us
that He must confess?

Abelard's Lovesong to Heloise

My heaven's love, my Heloise
As pure as sky, as God above
Thou art his strength, his power, his ease
thou art his sign, his perfect dove

Ah Heloise, o Heloise
the frantic beating of your love
is wings of praise to him above
whose soul thou art, my Heloise

Lift up my cheer, lift up my love
This crystal light, dark thoughts appease
Prise loose my soul, my Heloise
and let it drift to God above

Heloise, my Heloise
Light my darkness, from above
Take hold us both, and gently squeeze
the essence of our perfect love

My life, my joy, my Heloise
The living form of God above
Thou art his strength, his power to please
full promise of his perfect love

Erda's Song

Cold, shivering bones, but colder is my soul
Chill is the winter wind which blows
Chipped are my cheeks, and nibbled out my nose
By the scything wind, by the scything wind

Dark castle night, but darker yet my soul
No skein of light from the tower shows
Black shadows formed by my nameless woes
And the scything wind, o the scything wind

Weak, tumbling form, but weaker still my soul
As I wend and weave in this winter snow
No sight to see where we stumbling go
Through the scything wind, through the scything wind

Dark reaper Death, come strip my soul
Come sheave my claws, bind up these toes
My crop is cut, bleak harvest o'er
For the scything wind, for the scything wind

The Bishop's Dirty Ditty (with Hortensio & the Goliards)

HORTENSIO	There was a lover and and his lass *Sing heigh, sing heigh the high ho* And he did tickle her up her ass *Sing hey, the dirty Johnny*
EBERHARD	There's not a maid in Christendom did so enjoy such sitting as on dear John's stout pole she thrust the hatch she used for shitting
ALL	There was a lover and his lass *Sing heigh, sing heigh the high ho* And he did tickle her up her ass *Sing hey, the dirty Johnny*

HORTENSIO   She went to see her Bishop, dear
to make her dark confession
He growled with rage to hear her speak
and read his angry lesson

BISHOP   Of all your vows, this makes foul mock
To so be-crap your marriage!
Bend over, dear, and lift your smock
I'd better view the damage

HORTENSIO   She trembling did, and crossed herself
the Bishop hummed his Latin
and turning her the other way
he poked his little bat in

ALL   There was a lover and his lass
Sing heigh, sing heigh the high ho
And he did tickle her up her ass
Sing hey, the dirty Johnny

BISHOP   You see my dear, this is the gate
which God gave man in women
You'll feel God's finger pointing out
How pure 'tis to be swiven

HORTENSIO   She cried with joy, and angel's bliss
to be so sweet forgiven
I'll not let Johnny's faith rise up
unless I'm properly riven!

EBERHARD   Now John doth droop, and John doth weep
No more sweet tight-arsed friction
And fortune's gone, for he must keep
Ten children round his kitchen

ALL   There was a lover and his lass
Sing heigh, sing heigh the high ho
And he did tickle her up her ass
Sing hey, the dirty Johnny

Song of the Students

GRIMKIN
Now toil is done, let cool the forge
Lay up your tools, you chipsters there
Monks cease your chant, and awful dirge
Tomorrow dawns upon the Fair!

ALL
We'll goose the girls, we'll bait the bear
we'll sluice away life's ancient care
raw youth will rampage everywhere
about the Fair, about the Fair!

GRIMKIN
At morning Mass they'll sing the feast
'Twont worry me, I won't be there!
Who'd waste the day with shrivelled priest
Scab up his knees, and miss the Fair!

ALL
We'll lift the skirts of all that's fair
And pinch and rub what's hidden there
We'll tug the dewy, golden hair
of all sweet maidens at the Fair!

GRIMKIN
The troupsters will perform their work
and gobble fire, and leap in t'air
And all who watch them madly jerk
will squeal with joy at such a Fair!

ALL
Come drink a bumper, fill her up!
Let all alive rise up to swear
'Tis laughter best renews the cup
That's cold and hollow, 'til the Fair!

Goliards and the Troupster Girl

THISTLEDOWN There was a maid upon the road
and a merry, merry maid was she
she travelled far, she travelled free
and every dirty man what tackled her
she'd bite his balls
with a one, two, three
for her teeth were as sharp as blades, o!
The teeth of the dread, dread maid

EBERHARD And there was a songster on the road
and he sang so merrily
he wandered far, and he wandered free
and every little slut which ran at him
he'd box her cunt
with a one, two, three
for his prick was as thick as a spade, o!
He's the pick of the dread, dread maid

MICHAEL And the songster's mate trod the very same road
and a dear dear friend was he
he roamed with his friend in the land of the free
and he watched silly cows fall in love with him
and he'd slap their ears
with a one, two, three
for his jealousy filled him with rage, o!
and his fear of the dread, dread maid

THISTLEDOWN So off they set down the long and lonely road
MICHAEL and weren't they a pretty little three!
EBERHARD they wandered far, and they wandered free
MICHAEL and he would root the girl, whilst I did bugger him

ALL *with a one, two, three*
they played with their hot and lusty blades, o!
and they all took their turns at the maid

With a one, two three
they all took their turn at the maid!

170

Abelard's Song for Eberhard

Be soft with him, my gracious Lord
be generous, as with thy kin
he flutters wild, a wounded bird
don't buffet him, or scoff at him

As oft you hear his mocking word
be deaf with him, be blind to him
and as a mother rocks her child
so cosset him, breathe soft on him

He bears thy voice, he sings thy song
though raucous is his merry hymn
he hath not nestled overlong
in thy great hands, enfolding him

So gentle him, my gentle Lord
and set him loose to swoop and sing
Thou lift'st him high on fragile wing
thou mighty wind, be soft with him

Eberhard's Last Song, with Elise

EBERHARD   I felt a breath upon my cheek
             as smooth as silk, as swan's soft down
             It was a tear crept from my soul
             to smear the paint of a loveless clown

ELISE   I whispered close upon thy cheek
             'twas that thou felt there, trickling down
             I'll ever love thee, wandering man
             and smooth a pillow for my clown

EBERHARD   I'll ply thee treats with my mandola
             and sing thy praise in every town
             The whole wide world will trill the beauty
             of the cruel maid who spurned the clown

ELISE	Thou art but game, and game's thy art
	and pleasure 'tis, to sport thy round
	But we grow old, and teased apart
	and age does not become a clown
EBERHARD	I felt a breath upon my cheek
	as smooth as silk, as swan's soft down
	It was a tear crept out my soul
	to smear the paint of a loveless clown

Elise's Song for Abelard

O father mine, my Abelard
the seed you've sown is grown to tree
its slender branches spread to shade
your sleeping face, and cover thee

My life, my love, my Abelard
you brought the world alive for me
each wondrous flower, each note and word
in nature's magic harmony

Your soul is firm, as rock is hard
challenging eternity
yet ever gentle was your word
and never rock did grate on me

You taught my heart to weakly sing
Kind father dear, you handled me
with gentle fingers patched my wing
and like an angel set me free

Precious father, Abelard
Christ in you has victory
Yet glories not in being Lord
but murmurs hymns of love to thee

Appendix

The four poems here are connected to poems of mine in the foregoing collection, although each is a fine piece in itself, and worth preserving.

The first, 'The Dead' is by my grandfather, A.N.G. Irving, who served with the AIF in 1915-1917. This poem, with the other piece of his recorded here ('Poppy Day'), inspired my piece 'In Flanders Fields' (page 10), which is my tribute to him.

Irving was a splendid writer, and a wonderful man — indeed, he was the most gracious and civilised I have met. He farmed all his life in the Cranbrook district of Western Australia, and was a key player in the campaign lasting from the 1930's to the 1970's towards the introduction of the Reserve Price scheme for woolgrowers.

The third poem is the great Australian piece 'The Bastard from the Bush', attributed (in my view, correctly) to Henry Lawson. I have mimicked this piece on page 31 of this book.

The last is Sidney Keyes' lovely poem 'Remember Your Lovers', first published in the Oxford University undergraduate magazine 'The Cherwell', November 7th, 1940, with which my good friend John Harper-Nelson (who knew Keyes) was involved. Sidney Keyes was killed aged 20, in Tunisia during WWII. My tribute is on page 50.

The Dead

by A.N.G. Irving, and dated Passchendaele, 1919 (i.e. after the Armistice). Passchendaele was one of the charnel-house battlefields of World War One upon which Irving served, where thousands of lives were thrown away in a futile taking and re-taking of a strategically unimportant ridge.

Tread softly lest your feet disturb the dead
From their long sleep, and make them think once more
Of the green earth and blue sky overhead,
Or the wild waters breaking on the shore
Of some lone cove which once in life they knew
And loved, and left to pass into the fire.
Speak lightly, lest your voices, breaking through
Their age-long rest, shall wake them to desire.

Walk reverently. You tread on holy ground:
The ground from which the tender flowers start,
And raise their heads to heaven from the mound.
They draw their life from some dead hero's heart.
The strain of war is fading from the land;
Where once was tumbled earth is growing grass.
The crimson poppies bloom on every hand.
Ah! Step between the flowers as you pass.

Poppy Day

by A.N.G. Irving, written in the 1920's on Remembrance Day

Oh poppies glowing scarlet 'gainst the bosom of a maiden,
Of a maiden selling poppies to the mourners for the dead.
Were you gathered in a garden where the air was heavy laden
With the perfume of the jasmine and the roses white and red?

Did you turn your fairy faces to the sun in pleasant places?
Did you whisper scented secrets to the lily and the rose?
Did you greet the tender primrose in the garden which it graces?
Did you droop your heads in slumber when the day drew to a close?

I, too, have had a garden, and the tender plants I cherished
Were heavy with the promise of their tribute to the sun;
But an icy blast has swept it, and the fairest flowers have perished
And have broken from the branches ere their blooming was begun.

And the buds I saw unfolding, and the flowers that I tended
Have fallen in their glory, and have crumbled to decay.
They have vanished from the garden, and their glad, brief day is ended,
And the bursting buds are withered and their beauty passed away.

Poppies! Scarlet poppies! I will take you as a token.
I will lay you on the altar as the sacrifice of one
Who would pay a lowly tribute from a spirit bruised and broken
To a flaming flower that perished as it opened to the sun.

The Bastard from the Bush

by Henry Lawson (attributed), the model for my piece on page 31

As the night was falling slowly over city, town and bush,
From a slum in Jones' Alley came the Captain of the Push,
And his whistle loud and piercing woke the echoes of the Rocks,
And a dozen ghouls came slouching round the corners of the blocks.

Then the Captain jerked a finger at a stranger on the kerb
Whom he qualified politely with an adjective and verb.
Then he made the introduction: 'Here's a covey from the bush —
'Fuck me blind, he wants to join us — be a member of the Push.'

Then the stranger made this answer to the Captain of the Push,
'Why, fuck you dead, I'm foreskin Fred, the bastard from the bush.
'I've been in every two-up school from Darwin to the 'Loo,
'I've ridden colts and black gins — what more can a bastard do?'

'Are you game to smash a window?' asked the Captain of the Push.
'I'd knock a fucking house down,' said the bastard from the bush.
'Would you take a maiden's baby?' said the Captain of the Push.
'I'd take a baby's maiden,' said the bastard from the bush.

'Would you dong a bloody copper if you caught the cunt alone,
'Would you stoush a swell or Chinkee, split his garret with a stone?
'Would you have a moll to keep you, would you swear off work for good'
'What? Live on prostitution? My colonial oath I would!'

'Would you care to have a gasper?' said the Captain of the Push.
'I'll take the bloody packet,' said the bastard from the bush.
Then the Pushites all took counsel, saying, 'Fuck me, but he's game.
'Let's make him our star basher, he'll live up to his name.'

So they took him to their hideout, that bastard from the bush,
And they granted him all privileges appertaining to the Push.
But soon they found his little ways were more than they could stand,
And finally the Captain thus addressed his little band.

'Now listen here, you buggers, we've caught a fucking tartar,
'At every kind of bludging, that bastard is a starter,
'At poker and at two-up, he's shook our fucking rolls,
'He swipes our fucking liquor, and he robs our fucking molls.'

So down in Jones' Alley all the members of the Push
Laid a dark and dirty ambush for the bastard from the bush.
But against the wall of Riley's pub, the bastard made a stand,
A nasty grin upon his dial, a bike-chain in each hand.

They sprang upon him in a bunch, but one by one they fell,
With crack of bone, unearthly groan, and agonising yell,
Till the sorely battered Captain, spitting teeth and gouts of blood,
Held an ear all torn and bleeding in a hand bedaubed with mud.

'You low polluted bastard,' snarled the Captain of the Push,
'Get back to where your sort belong, that's somewhere in the bush:
'And I hope heaps of misfortune may soon tumble down on you,
'May some lousy harlot dose you till your bollocks turn sky-blue.

'May the pangs of windy spasms through your bowels dart,
'May you shit your bloody trousers every time you try to fart,
'May you take a swig of gin's piss, mistaking it for beer,
'May the next push you impose on toss you out upon your ear.

'May the itching piles torment you, may corns grow on your feet,
'May crabs as big as spiders attack your balls a treat,
'Then when you're down and outed, to a hopeless bloody wreck,
'May you slip back through your arsehole, and break your fucking neck.'

Remember Your Lovers

by Sidney Keyes

Young men walking the open streets
Of death's republic, remember your lovers.

When you foresaw with vision prescient
The planet pain rising across your sky
We fused your sight in our soft-burning beauty
We laid you down in meadows drunk with cowslips
And led you in the ways of our bright city.
Young men who wander death's vague meadows,
Remember your lovers who gave you more than flowers.

When truth came prying like a surgeon's knife
Among the delicate movements of your brain,
We called your spirit from its narrow den
And kissed your courage back to meet the blade —
Our anaesthetic beauty saved you then.
Young men whose sickness death has cured at last,
Remember your lovers and cover their disease.

When you woke grave-chilled at midnight
To pace the pavement of your bitter dream,
We brought you back to bed, and brought you home
From the dark antechamber of desire
Into our lust as warm as candle-flame.
Young men who lie in the carven beds of death,
Remember your lovers who gave you more than dreams.

From the sun sheltering your careless head
Or from the painted devil your quick eye,
We led you out of terror tenderly
And fooled you into peace with our soft words,
And gave you all we had and let you die.

Young men, drunk with death's unquenchable wisdom,
Remember your lovers who gave you more than love.